KINGS & QUEENS
OF ANCIENT BRITAIN

de bello ubi tumpharat fundau. Regnau anis xxvi. z ap'lus

Aula westm gstrur. tande sagta puit p'cm vernaua

m Rer
e p'm p'co
onem el

ucus se
Rer cu
ccc ccc

enricus vir potens z sapiens Iurau leges sci eduuardi iiii

Iste Stephanus miles strenuissim omib; dieb;

KINGS & QUEENS
OF ANCIENT BRITAIN

A magnificent chronicle of the first rulers of the British Isles, from the time of Boudicca and King Arthur to the Wars of the Roses, the Crusades and the reign of Richard III

CHARLES PHILLIPS
CONSULTANT: DR JOHN HAYWOOD FRHS

southwater

This edition is published by Southwater, an imprint of Anness Publishing Ltd, Hermes House, 88–89 Blackfriars Road, London SE1 8HA; tel. 020 7401 2077; fax 020 7633 9499

www.southwaterbooks.com; www.annesspublishing.com

Anness Publishing has a new picture agency outlet for images for publishing, promotions or advertising. Please visit our website www.practicalpictures.com for more information.

UK agent: The Manning Partnership Ltd; tel. 01225 478444; fax 01225 478440; sales@manning-partnership.co.uk
UK distributor: Grantham Book Services Ltd; tel. 01476 541080; fax 01476 541061; orders@gbs.tbs-ltd.co.uk
North American agent/distributor: National Book Network; tel. 301 459 3366; fax 301 429 5746; www.nbnbooks.com
Australian agent/distributor: Pan Macmillan Australia; tel. 1300 135 113; fax 1300 135 103; customer.service@macmillan.com.au
New Zealand agent/distributor: David Bateman Ltd; tel. (09) 415 7664; fax (09) 415 8892

Publisher: Joanna Lorenz
Senior Managing Editor: Conor Kilgallon
Editor: Joy Wotton
Consultants: Dr John Haywood, Stephen Slater
Designer: Nigel Partridge
Illustrators: Anthony Duke and Rob Highton
Production Controller: Lee Sargent

ETHICAL TRADING POLICY
At Anness Publishing we believe that business should be conducted in an ethical and ecologically sustainable way, with respect for the environment and a proper regard to the replacement of the natural resources we employ.
As a publisher, we use a lot of wood pulp to make high-quality paper for printing, and that wood commonly comes from spruce trees. We are therefore currently growing more than 500,000 trees in two Scottish forest plantations near Aberdeen – Berrymoss (130 hectares/320 acres) and West Touxhill (125 hectares/305 acres). The forests we manage contain twice the number of trees employed each year in paper-making for our books.

Because of this ongoing ecological investment programme, you, as our customer, can have the pleasure and reassurance of knowing that a tree is being cultivated on your behalf to naturally replace the materials used to make the book you are holding.

Our forestry programme is run in accordance with the UK Woodland Assurance Scheme (UKWAS) and will be certified by the internationally recognized Forest Stewardship Council (FSC). The FSC is a non-government organization dedicated to promoting responsible management of the world's forests. Certification ensures forests are managed in an environmentally sustainable and socially responsible basis. For further information about this scheme, go to www.annesspublishing.com/trees

Previously published as part of a larger volume, *The Complete Illustrated Guide to the Kings & Queens of Britain*

p. 1 Windsor Castle. p. 2 William I, William II, Henry I and Stephen. p. 3 The Imperial State Crown. pp. 4–5 (top): shields of William I, Stephen, Henry II, Edward III, the House of Stewart, Richard II, Henry IV. (bottom): coins of Edgar of Wessex, Aethelred of Wessex, Cnut of the Danes, Edward I of England, Henry VI of England, Edward IV of England, Henry VI of England and Richard III of England.

CONTENTS

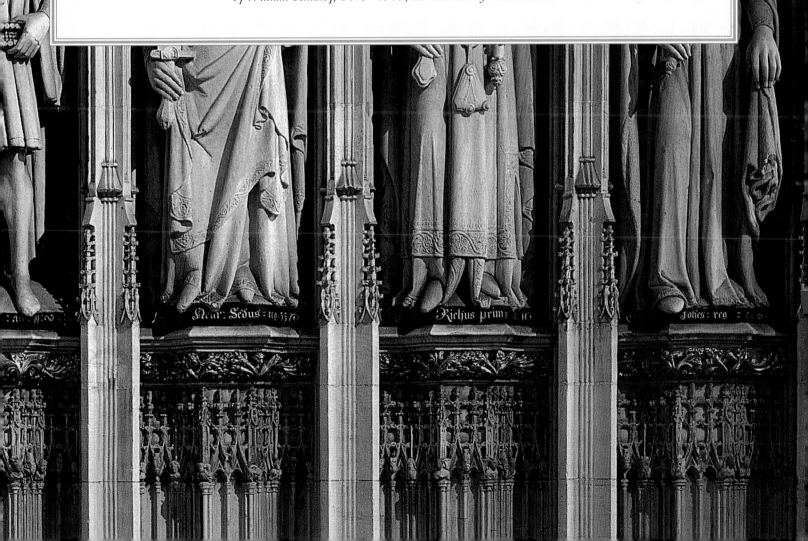

ANCIENT MONARCHS

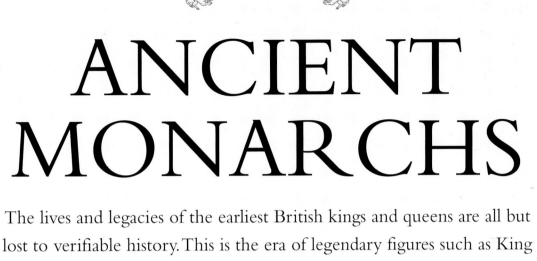

The lives and legacies of the earliest British kings and queens are all but lost to verifiable history. This is the era of legendary figures such as King Arthur, famed lord of Camelot. Their successors among ancient and medieval monarchs include well-documented rulers, men of deathless renown – such as Alfred the Great, who defeated the Vikings in 871 and promoted English learning; Robert I the Bruce, hero of the 1314 Battle of Bannockburn; and Henry V of England, icon of English nationalism.

Left: Statues of the kings of England from William the Conqueror to King John,
by William Hindley, 1473–1505, the cathedral of York Minster.

INTRODUCTION

The English word 'king' derives from the Germanic *cyning/kuning*, imported by Anglo-Saxon raiders who sailed across the North Sea to invade England in the 5th and 6th centuries AD. In modern usage, the word usually means a supreme ruler, with sovereign authority over an independent state.

Britain certainly had 'kings', in the sense of supreme rulers, before Anglo-Saxon times. The first we know by name are those who faced the Roman invasions of 55/54BC and then AD43, tribal leaders such as Cassivellaunus and Caratacus, rulers of the Catuvellauni of southern England. In this era and that of the early Anglo-Saxons, kings were warrior leaders who held power primarily on the basis of force. The consequence of this was that when a warrior-king died, his kingdom often died with him – there was little if no belief in a hereditary right to rule. A kingdom was only as strong as its king, but very slowly the idea of an inherited right to rule began to develop – not

Below: William the Conqueror began building the White Tower in 1066. It became a part of the Tower of London.

Above: Edward the Confessor's body is carried to Westminster Abbey, in a detail from the Bayeux Tapestry (1082).

necessarily through a dynasty of blood relations, but at least through a king's designation of his chosen successor. This introduced the idea of a ruler's legitimacy – force of arms alone was no longer all.

By the 7th century, Christianity was taking root in Britain. As the religion spread after the conversion in *c.*AD600 of King Aethelbert of Kent, the first Anglo-Saxon monarch to become Christian, so the idea developed of divine election – kings were presented as God's chosen instruments, with a special capacity to bring God's blessing to the kingdom and its people. As the Christian God was King of Heaven, bringing justice and showering blessings on the needy, so the king on earth brought similar if less glorious benefits to his people. Kings were, like priests, servants of the Lord: the ordination-coronation in 973 of King Edgar, in which he was anointed with holy oil, brought out this point explicitly.

THE RISE OF 'PARLIAMENT'
From the time of England's Anglo-Saxon kingdoms, monarchs sought to establish and extend their authority through the rule of the king's law. To

this end the Anglo-Saxon kings relied on the support of the king's council or Witan. This body, which consisted of leading nobles and churchmen, was summoned by the king to advise him, to approve new laws, to attest royal grants of land and to back him when confronting rebels. The Witan legitimized the king's actions, his rule and even his accession – in theory Witan members elected the king, although in practice this was a matter of approving a *fait accompli*. Even though the role and person of Anglo-Saxon monarchs remained to a large extent in the Germanic tradition of king as warrior-leader, the king's power was stabilized by the role of the Witan.

From the 11th century the Witan's successor, the *commune concilium* of Anglo-Norman kings, performed the same role: the king ruled with full authority, given the consent of his barons. These men, the principal landowners, were formally bound to the monarch in a subordinate position through the ties of the feudal system. In the 13th century, the barons asserted their power in the face of abuses of royal authority – forcing the agreement of King John to the Magna Carta, a charter guaranteeing the 'liberties' of leading subjects, in 1215. In earlier years, Henry I, King Stephen and Henry II had all issued charters, but these had been granted by royal will; the Magna Carta was the first charter imposed upon the king by barons threatening civil war – it contained a clause empowering a baronial council of 25 men to take up arms against the king should he fail to abide by the terms.

In the reign of John's son Henry III the barons were increasingly angered by the king's reliance on French advisers following his marriage to Eleanor of Provence and imposed significant limits on royal power by forcing Henry to agree to the Provisions of Oxford in 1258. Under this agreement a privy council of 15 members, appointed by the barons, was established to control government. Henry later renounced the Provisions, leading to a civil war in which he was briefly deposed, and power passed into the hands of nobleman Simon de Montfort in 1263.

Below: Built by Edward IV in 1475, St George's Chapel, within Windsor Castle, has been the burial place of many kings.

Above: Dunstan of Canterbury (AD924–88) was a monastic reformer as well as the creator of royal ordination–coronation rites.

While in power de Montfort called a widely representative governmental council, which in addition to clerics and barons included two knights from each shire and two burgesses from each borough. Henry III's son, Prince Edward, defeated de Montfort in 1265 at Evesham and subsequently ruled with great authority as King Edward I. Yet even he was reliant on the support of a council of advisers, principally to

Above: The legitimate son of Henry I (1100–35) died in 1120. Henry's nephew and daughter disputed the succession.

approve taxation to fund his military campaigns against the Scots and Welsh.

Around this time the council began to be called 'Parliament' (from the Old French *parlement*, 'a talk'). Edward I summoned combined meetings of the *Magnum Concilium* ('Major Council', mainly of churchmen and magnates) and *Curia Regis* ('Royal Court', of lay advisers). Some meetings of the *Curia Regis* became known as *Concilium Regis in Parliamento* ('Royal Council in Parliament'). To some meetings Edward called knights and burgesses. The one in 1295 is generally labelled the 'Model Parliament' and identified as the first representative English parliament: in addition to magnates and leading churchmen, it included representatives of lesser clergy, a pair of knights from each county, two burgesses from every borough and two citizens of every city.

Thereafter for some 400 years the king ruled through Parliament. He could call it and dismiss it at will. Members of Parliament were by no means independent of royal power – and individuals might be imprisoned or put to death for overstepping the mark.

POMP AND PAGEANTRY

Public royal ceremony celebrates the ruling king or queen as the kingdom's most majestic individual, elevated far above even the proudest and noblest of subjects. Across centuries, the monarchy has emphasized its pre-eminence through a wide range of magnificent ceremonies – including ordination-coronation rites, royal weddings and funerals, reviews of the armed forces, triumphal processions or 'progresses' and elaborate social activities at court.

CORONATION CEREMONIAL

The coronation of King Edgar in Bath on 11 May 973 was the first at which an English monarch was anointed with oil. The ceremony emphasized Edgar's sacred calling and was deliberately reminiscent of a priest's ordination: it was delayed until the 14th year of Edgar's reign, when the king reached the age of 30, then the minimum for a priest. It was matched by a public celebration of Edgar's earthly supremacy, which took place at Chester later in the summer of 973: eight British monarchs recognized Edgar's pre-eminence and then rowed him across the River Dee from his palace in Chester to the Church of St John the Baptist on the

other bank. A small fleet of lesser ships carried leading noblemen behind him.

In 1485 Henry VII, the founder of the Tudor dynasty, held a coronation ceremony of the utmost splendour. It followed the tradition established by King Edgar and the new king and his followers wore magnificent robes.

The kings of Hanover maintained magnificent coronation ceremonies. George IV spent some £240,000 celebrating his coronation in 1820. Such

Above: The gold used in St Edward's Crown may have come from Edward the Confessor's crown. The Sceptre with the Cross contains the world's largest top-quality cut diamond, the Cullinan I. The Sceptre with the Dove, the Orb and the Ring are also shown.

extravagant celebrations led to a backlash – William IV had a deliberately low-key coronation in 1831 – but from the late Victorian period onwards pomp and glory returned. In 1911 King George V was lavishly crowned twice – once in Westminster Abbey in London and once in India, as its Emperor.

BRITAIN'S CROWN JEWELS

The Crown Jewels are kept in the Jewel House at the Tower of London. The jewels have had a troubled history. The first monarch to collect royal regalia was probably Edward the Confessor, but this first collection was lost by King John in quicksand as he tried to cross the Wash, a tidal estuary in

Left: Edinburgh Castle dominates the skyline, just as it has dominated Scottish history as a stronghold and seat of kings.

eastern England, in 1216. A replacement set was made, but following the execution of Charles I Oliver Cromwell ordered its destruction. Then another new set was made at a cost of £12,185 for the Restoration of the Monarchy in 1660, although some earlier pieces – such as the 12th-century Coronation Spoon – were recovered and returned to Charles II.

At the climax of the coronation service, after taking the coronation oath and being anointed with holy oil using the Coronation Spoon, the monarch is handed the Sovereign's Orb, fitted with the Coronation Ring, given the Sceptre with the Cross and the Sceptre with the Dove and then crowned with St Edward's Crown. Most of these treasures date to the Restoration; but the gold in St Edward's Crown may have come from Edward the Confessor's crown and the Coronation Ring is from William IV's crowning in 1831. On leaving Westminster Abbey at the end of the coronation and at the annual State Opening of Parliament, the monarch wears the Imperial State Crown, made in 1937 for George VI's coronation.

FUNERAL RITES

Another lavish event as a reign begins is the celebration of the previous monarch's life with a funeral procession and burial in an elaborate tomb. In times of disputed successions, an imposing funeral could make a public statement, suggesting a new ruler was a suitable successor. For example, on the day of his own coronation (6 January 1066), Harold II held a funeral procession for Edward the Confessor, who was buried before the High Altar in Westminster Abbey, the church he had established. The procession is shown on the Bayeux Tapestry.

In the early years of the Tudor dynasty Henry VIII laid on a grand state funeral for his father Henry VII, with a procession of 600 candle-bearers, the royal choir, and a host of churchmen. In 1901, Edward VII paid tribute to his revered mother Queen Victoria with the grandest of funerals. After the funeral in St George's

Chapel, she lay in state for two days, before being buried at Frogmore. Almost exactly 101 years later, Queen Elizabeth the Queen Mother was remembered by her daughter Queen Elizabeth II in a grand state funeral at Westminster Abbey on 9 April 2002. She lay in state in Westminster Hall from 5-8 April and was carried in procession to the abbey – with around 1 million people lining the route – for her funeral.

ROYAL WEDDINGS

Because they have often brought about the union of two ruling houses, royal weddings have required magnificent ceremony – not only to impress the people, but also to honour the king or queen's new royal in-laws. Richard II married Princess Isabella of France, daughter of France's King Charles VI, amid great splendour at Calais in 1396. A little over 100 years later, when King James IV of Scotland married Princess Margaret of England, daughter of King

Above: The west front of Westminster Abbey, which has seen the coronations and funerals of many English and British monarchs.

Henry VII, on 8 August 1503, celebrations at Holyrood Palace in Edinburgh included pageants, jousting tournaments and wine-fuelled banquets – and the marriage was marked by the publication of the poem "The Thistle and the Rose", by leading Scots poet William Dunbar. In the modern era, the wedding of Prince Charles to Lady Diana Spencer on 30 July 1981 was a glittering celebration of romance and royal splendour.

In the modern era, in which kings and queens have lost real power, coronations, weddings, funerals and other aspects of royal pageantry – such as Elizabeth II's Silver and Golden Jubilee celebrations, the Trooping of the Colour and State Opening of Parliament – have assumed importance as symbolic enactments of the greatness of the country's and the monarchy's history.

TIMELINE OF ANCIENT MONARCHS

55BC–AD799

55BC Cassivellaunus, of the Catuvellauni tribe, is the first named British king. He leads opposition to the invasions of Roman Emperor Julius Caesar.

*c.***10BC** Tasciovanus, King of the Catuvellauni, mints a coin bearing his name and face. He is the earliest British king whose name appears on a coin.

AD10–41 Tasciovanus's successor is Cunobelinus. The Roman historian Suetonius (AD69–*c.*125) later refers to Cunobelinus as *rex Britannorum* ('King of the Britons').

AD43 Cunobelinus's son, Caratacus, is a leader of British resistance to a Roman invasion led by the Emperor Claudius.

AD60 Boudicca of the Iceni tribe leads an uprising against Roman rule.

*c.***AD450–550** Anglo-Saxon invaders gain control of south-east England and use it as a base for westward expansion.

*c.***AD500** The warrior-leader Ambrosius Aurelianus leads Celtic tribes to victory over Saxon incomers at Mount Badon. His exploits are probably the basis for the legend of King Arthur.

*c.***AD600** By this date there are seven main Anglo-Saxon kingdoms: the kingdoms of Northumbria, Mercia, East Anglia, Kent, Wessex, Sussex and Essex.

*c.***AD600** Aethelbert of Kent is the first Anglo-Saxon king to become Christian.

AD757–96 Offa, ruler of Mercia, declares himself 'King of the English'. His territory includes Sussex, Kent, East Anglia and most of Wessex in addition to Mercia. He builds a 240-km (150-mile) non-continuous barrier – 'Offa's Dyke' – along Mercia's border with Wales.

AD786 The first Viking raid on Britain hits Portland, Wessex.

AD787 Egfrith of Mercia is the first English king to be anointed at his coronation. The ceremony takes place while his father, Offa, is still on the throne. It is carried out by a papal legate during a visit to Mercia.

AD800–1016

AD838 King Egbert of Wessex defeats a combined Cornish and Viking army at Hingston Down, Cornwall. In the course of his reign (802–39), Egbert makes Wessex the pre-eminent Anglo-Saxon kingdom, incorporating Sussex, Kent and Essex.

AD843 King Kenneth mac Alpin of the Scots (840-47) creates the Scottish-Pictish kingdom of Alba and rules as King of the Scots and Picts 847-58.

AD869 Viking warriors Ubba and Ingvar defeat and kill the Christian King Edmund of East Anglia at Hoxne, Suffolk. Edmund is afterwards celebrated as a saint.

May AD878 King Alfred the Great forces the Vikings to sue for peace after a major victory at Edington, Salisbury Plain. Alfred's coins recognize him as *rex Anglorum* ('King of all the English').

AD934–9 Athelstan is the first king to rule all of England.

AD973 For the crowning of Edgar of Wessex, the Archbishop of Canterbury, Dunstan, develops a coronation service – incorporating the anointing of the king with oil – that has endured in various forms into the 21st century.

Apr 1016 King Cnut and King Edmund Ironside divide England on the death of King Aethelred.

30 Nov 1016 Edmund Ironside's death leaves Cnut ruling alone. This marks the beginning of the Danish line of English kings.

Above: William I of England.

1017–1065

1019 Cnut becomes King of Denmark and England becomes part of a Scandinavian empire.

1035 King Cnut dies. His illegitimate son Harold 'Harefoot' usurps the throne intended for Cnut's legitimate son Harthacnut. Harold is crowned King Harold I of England.

1040 Harold I dies and is succeeded by Harthacnut.

14 Aug 1040 Macbeth succeeds Duncan I as King of Scotland.

8 June 1042 On Harthacnut's death the crown passes to his half-brother, Edward the Confessor. This restores the throne to the House of Wessex, whose rule began with King Egbert (827–39).

1052 Edward the Confessor begins work on Westminster Abbey.

Above: Edgar of Wessex.

Above: Aethelred of Wessex.

1066–1167

5 Jan 1066 Edward the Confessor dies, resulting in a succession crisis with rival claimants including Harold Godwineson, earl of Wessex, and William, duke of Normandy.

6 Jan 1066 Harold Godwineson is crowned King Harold II of England,

14 Oct 1066 Duke William of Normandy defeats Harold II in the Battle of Hastings and claims the throne as King William I of England. He is the first of the Norman kings of England.

1087 Following the death of William I in Normandy, his middle son claims the throne as William II and defeats rebels seeking to replace him with William I's eldest son Robert Curthose.

2 Aug 1100 William II is killed while hunting in the New Forest, Hampshire. His younger brother, Henry, claims the throne as Henry I.

1120 Henry's only two legitimate male heirs, Princes William and Henry, drown when the White Ship sinks in the Channel as the royal party is returning from France to England.

1127 Henry names his daughter Matilda, wife of the Holy Roman Emperor Henry V, as his heir.

1 Dec 1135 Henry I dies.

1135-53 Matilda and Henry I's nephew, Stephen, dispute the throne. Stephen is twice crowned King of England.

1149 King David I rules a Scotland that extends as far south as the river Tees.

1154 Under the terms of the 1153 Treaty of Wallingford, the Empress Matilda's son – Henry Plantagenet – succeeds to the English throne on the death of Stephen as Henry II. He founds the royal house of Plantagenet.

June 1162 Henry appoints Thomas à Becket Archbishop of Canterbury

1163 Owain Gwynedd, King of Gwynedd, is honoured as 'Prince of Wales' in a treaty that recognizes Henry II of England as his feudal overlord.

Above: Stephen of England.

1168–1198

1168 William the Lion of Scots makes an alliance with Louis VII of France. Some see this as the beginning of the centuries-long 'Auld Alliance' between Scotland and France.

29 Dec 1170 Perhaps on Henry II's orders, Thomas à Becket is murdered in Canterbury Cathedral. Becket is named a saint within 18 months.

1189 Henry II dies and is succeeded by his son, Richard I.

12 May 1191 In Cyprus, while en route to the Holy Land to join the Third Crusade (1190–2), Richard I marries Berengaria of Navarre.

1193 After being captured by Holy Roman Emperor Henry VI, Richard I is freed on payment of a king's ransom of 150,000 marks.

Above: Cnut of the Danes.

Above: Henry II of England.

1199–1215

6 April 1199 Having spent only six months of his reign in England, Richard I dies at Châlus, Limousin, France, and is succeeded by his brother, John.

1204 England loses almost all her possessions in France.

Nov 1209 Following a dispute, John refuses to accept the papal nominee Stephen Langton as Archbishop of Canterbury and is excommunicated by Pope Innocent III.

1210 John defeats an Irish revolt.

20 July 1213 After accepting Stephen Langton as Archbishop of Canterbury, King John is formally absolved of his excommunication.

1215 King John signs Magna Carta, a charter of liberties imposed on him by leading barons.

Above: Edward I of England.

Above: Edward III of England.

Above: The House of Stewart.

1216–1269

1216 Llywelyn ap Iorwerth, prince of Gwynedd, unites Wales under his rule.

18 Oct 1216 John dies at Newark, after losing the crown jewels when crossing the Wash, a tidal estuary in eastern England.

28 Oct 1216 King John's successor, the nine-year-old Henry III, is crowned king in a makeshift ceremony at Gloucester.

17 May 1220 Henry has a second coronation, in Westminster Abbey.

14 Jan 1236 Henry marries Eleanor of Provence.

1240 Henry recognizes Dafydd ap Llywelyn of Gwynedd as the 'paramount prince in Wales'.

1265 Henry's son Edward defeats Simon de Montfort at Evesham, crushing a baronial revolt led by de Montfort.

1270–1299

16 Nov 1272 Henry III dies in London and is succeeded by Prince Edward as King Edward I.

19 Aug 1274 Edward I is crowned king in Westminster Abbey.

1284 After putting down Welsh revolts, Edward I imposes English rule in Wales.

1290 Edward I is distraught at the death of his wife Eleanor of Castile: he builds 12 memorial crosses to mark the places where her funeral cortège stopped en route to Westminster Abbey in London from her place of death, Harby in Nottinghamshire.

1290 Queen Margaret of Scotland, the 'Maid of Norway', dies aged seven on her way to Scotland.

1292 John Balliol is elected King of Scotland by Edward I of England.

1300–1369

1300 Edward I, 'the Hammer of the Scots', removes the ancient Scottish-Pictish coronation stone to London and makes it part of his coronation chair in a calculated insult to Scottish pride.

7 Feb 1301 Edward I's son Edward is created the first English 'Prince of Wales'.

23 Aug 1305 Edward I executes Scottish rebel William Wallace.

27 Mar 1306 Robert 'the Bruce' is invested as Robert I of Scots at Scone.

7 July 1307 Edward I dies of dysentery at Burgh by Sands, near Carlisle, and is succeeded by his son as Edward II.

24 June 1314 Robert I defeats Edward II of England at Bannockburn.

6 Apr 1320 Leading Scottish nobles proclaim Scotland's independence from England in the Declaration of Arbroath.

1327 Edward II, imprisoned by Queen Isabella and Mortimer, is forced to abdicate and is horribly murdered.

1 Feb 1327 Edward II's son is crowned Edward III in Westminster Abbey.

1340 Edward III declares himself King of France.

26 Aug 1346 Edward defeats the French at Crécy. His son Edward, Prince of Wales, kills the King of Bohemia and takes as his own the king's emblem of three feathers and motto *Ich Dien* ('I serve').

1346-57 Edward III holds King David II of Scots in captivity for 11 years.

24 June 1348 Edward founds the knightly fellowship of the Most Noble Order of the Garter.

Above: Henry VI of England coat of arms.

Above: James III of Scotland.

Above: Henry VI of England salut d'or.

1370–1414

26 Mar 1371 After the death of King David II of Scots, his nephew Robert Stewart is crowned Robert II at Scone, and founds the royal house of Stewart.

21 June 1377 Edward III dies and is succeeded by his grandson, Richard II.

1381 Richard II faces down the Peasants' Revolt.

1387 Leading barons issue an appeal to the king to rid himself of his favourites Robert de Vere and the Earl of Suffolk. The rebel barons are subsequently known as the 'Lords Appellant'.

1395 Richard receives the submission of 80 Irish chiefs.

1397 Richard arranges the murder of Gloucester and the execution of Gloucester's ally, Arundel.

1398 Richard sends another Lord Appellant, Henry Bolingbroke, into exile.

30 Sep 1399 Richard II is deposed in Parliament. Henry Bolingbroke is acclaimed as king in his place.

13 Oct 1399 Henry Bolingbroke is crowned King Henry IV. He founds the House of Lancaster, a cadet or junior line of the House of Plantagenet.

21 July 1403 Henry IV defeats rebels at the Battle of Shrewsbury.

1406 Henry IV develops a mystery illness – leprosy?

1409 Henry IV captures Harlech Castle to end a long-running Welsh revolt.

20 March 1413 Henry IV dies at Westminster and is succeeded by his son as Henry V.

Above: Richard II of England.

Above: Henry IV of England.

1415–1435

1415 Henry V leads the English army to a victory over the French at Agincourt.

21 May 1420 Under the Treaty of Troyes, Henry V becomes Regent of France and heir to the French king, Charles VI.

2 June 1420 Henry marries Katherine, daughter of Charles VI, King of France.

6 Dec 1421 Henry and Katherine's son, also named Henry, is born at Windsor Castle and designated Duke of Cornwall.

31 Aug 1422 Henry V dies at the Castle of Bois-de-Vincennes, France. He is succeeded by his infant son.

6 Nov 1429 Henry VI's coronation is held in Westminster Abbey.

16 Dec 1431 Aged only 10, Henry VI is crowned Henri II, King of France, in Notre Dame de Paris.

1436–1485

1436 Charles VI of France captures Paris from the English.

July 1453 French victory over the English at Castillon leaves England with only one remaining French possession: Calais.

1455–85 During the reigns of Henry VI (1422–61; 1470–1), Edward IV (1461–70; 1471–83) and Richard III (1483–5), the rival houses of York and Lancaster contest the throne in the Wars of the Roses.

28 June 1461 Edward IV crowned at Westminster Abbey.

1485 The Lancastrian claimant, Henry Tudor, wins the crown in battle at Bosworth Field, killing King Richard III, and marries Elizabeth of York, daughter of the late King Edward IV.

Above: Edward IV of England.

Above: Robert III of Scotland.

Above: Richard III of England.

THE MONARCHS

This list of monarchs names the kings and queens of Britain from the time of the ancient rulers of England and Scotland to the present day.

Much of the monarchy's authority and prestige derives from its ancient roots, from the centuries of historical continuity celebrated in genealogical and dynastic tables. Yet there are countless examples of force of arms and political manoeuvring intervening in dynastic or designated succession. In 1066, Duke William of Normandy famously had to enforce his claim that he was the designated successor of King Edward the Confessor in the face of several rival claims, including that of Harold Godwine, Earl of Wessex, who had himself declared King Harold II and was crowned on the very day after Edward the Confessor's death. William's claim triumphed at the Battle of Hastings.

The great Scottish national hero Robert the Bruce killed his chief rival to the succession, John Comyn, before having himself crowned King Robert I of Scots. Richard III of England occupied the throne at the expense of his uncrowned nephew, the 12-year-old King Edward V, whom Richard almost certainly had murdered in the Tower of London. King Henry VII won the English crown in battle against King Richard III.

Throughout these and many other upheavals, the theory of dynastic succession with God's blessing was maintained and all these kings – usurpers or murderers as they might be – laid claim to a dynastic link and were anointed as God's chosen servants on the throne. Henry IV, a usurper, brought an innovation to the coronation in an attempt to legitimize his rule. His ordination was the first to use holy oil reputedly given to Saint Thomas à Becket by the Virgin Mary.

KINGS AND QUEENS OF SCOTLAND (TO 1603)

THE HOUSE OF MACALPINE
Kenneth I mac Alpin 841–859
Donald I 859–863
Constantine I 863–877
Aed Whitefoot 877–878
Eochaid 878–889 (joint)
Giric 878–889
Donald II Dasachtach 889–900
Constantine II 900–943
Malcolm I 943–954
Indulf 954–962
Dubh 962–967
Culen 967–971
Kenneth II 971–995
Constantine III 995–997
Kenneth III 997–1005
Malcolm II 1005–1034

THE HOUSE OF DUNKELD
Duncan I 1034–1040
Macbeth 1040–1057
Lulach 1057–1058
Malcolm III Canmore 1058–1093
Donald III 1093–1094
Duncan II 1094
Donald III 1094–1097 (joint)

Above: James IV of Scotland presenting arms to his wife Queen Margaret, daughter of King Henry VII of England.

Edmund 1094–1097 (joint)
Edgar 1097–1107
Alexander I 1107–1124
David I 1124–1153
Malcolm IV the Maiden 1153–1165
William I the Lion 1165–1214
Alexander II 1214–1249
Alexander III 1249–1286
Margaret, Maid of Norway 1286–1290

THE HOUSE OF BALLIOL
John Balliol 1292–1296

THE HOUSE OF BRUCE
Robert I the Bruce 1306–1329
David II 1329–1332, 1338–1371

THE HOUSE OF BALLIOL
Edward Balliol 1332–1336

THE HOUSE OF STEWART
Robert II 1371–1390
Robert III 1390–1406
James I 1406–1437
James II 1437–1460
James III 1460–1488
James IV 1488–1513
James V 1513–1542
Mary, Queen of Scots 1542–1567
James VI 1567–1603

Below: King David II of Scotland (left) makes peace with King Edward III of England, in 1357.

KINGS AND QUEENS OF ENGLAND

THE HOUSE OF WESSEX
Egbert (802–839)
Aethelwulf (839–858)
Aethelbald (858–860)
Aethelbert (860–865/6)
Aethelred I (865/6–871)
Alfred the Great (871–899)
Edward the Elder (899–924/5)
Athelstan (924/5–939)
Edmund I (939–946)
Eadred (946–955)
Eadwig (955–959)
Edgar (959–975)
Edward the Martyr (975–978)
Aethelred II the Unready (978–1013, 1014–1016)
Edmund Ironside (1016)

THE DANISH LINE
Cnut (1016–1035)
Harald I Hardrada (1035–1040)
Harthacnut (1040–1042)

THE HOUSE OF WESSEX, RESTORED
Edward the Confessor (1042–1066)
Harold II (1066)

THE NORMANS
William I the Conqueror (1066–1087)
William II Rufus (1087–1100)
Henry I (1100–1135)
Stephen (1135–1154)

Above: King John goes riding. Hunting was the sport of kings from William I.

THE PLANTAGENETS
Henry II (1154–1189)
Richard I the Lionheart (1189–1199)
John (1199–1216)
Henry III (1216–1272)
Edward I (1272–1307)
Edward II (1307–1327)
Edward III (1327–1377)
Richard II (1377–1399)

THE HOUSE OF LANCASTER
Henry IV (1399–1413)
Henry V (1413–1422)
Henry VI (1422–1461, 1470–1471)

THE HOUSE OF YORK
Edward IV (1461–1470, 1471–1483)
Edward V (1483)
Richard III (1483–1485)

THE HOUSE OF TUDOR
Henry VII (1485–1509)
Henry VIII (1509–1547)
Edward VI (1547–1553)
Lady Jane Grey (1553)
Mary I (1553–1558)
Elizabeth I (1558–1603)

Left: The heraldic badges of Kings Edward III, Richard II and Henry IV from Writhe's Garter Book.

KINGS AND QUEENS OF GREAT BRITAIN

THE HOUSE OF STUART
James I (1603-1625)
Charles I (1625-1649)
Charles II (1660-1685)
James II (1685-1688)
William III and Mary II (1689-1694)
William III (1689-1702)
Anne (1702-1714)

THE HOUSE OF HANOVER
George I (1714-1727)
George II (1727-1760)
George III (1760-1820)
George IV (1820-1830)
William IV (1830-1837)
Victoria (1837-1901)

THE HOUSE OF SAXE-COBURG-GOTHA
Edward VII (1901-1910)

THE HOUSE OF WINDSOR
George V (1910-1936)
Edward VIII (1936)
George VI (1936-1952)
Elizabeth II (1952-)

Below: The Archbishop of Canterbury reverently places the crown on George V's head at the coronation in 1911.

CHAPTER ONE

BOUDICCA TO STEPHEN

TO 1154

The origins of the British monarchy are shrouded in legend. The 12th-century Welsh churchman and chronicler Geoffrey of Monmouth produced, in his *Historia regum Britanniae* ('History of the Kings of Britain', *c.*1135–9), a chronology of 76 kings of Britain descended from the island's supposed first settlers: Brutus, great-grandson of Aeneas of Troy and his fellow-Trojan Corineus, who gave his name to Cornwall. Geoffrey claimed that he translated his chronicle from 'a very old book in the British tongue', but in truth the *Historia* was a combination of oral history, folklore, legend and the writer's invention.

Monmouth's chronology contains many romantic tales of famous kings, such as King Leir (the original of Shakespeare's *King Lear*), King Coel ('Old King Cole', supposedly the King of the Britons in the 3rd century and the grandfather of the Roman emperor Constantine the Great), and King Lud (said to have given his name to London). Lud's tale brings us to the beginning of true royal history for, according to Geoffrey, Lud was the brother of Cassivellaunus, an historical figure who fought against Julius Caesar's invaders in 54BC. Because of their encounters with the literate Romans, who wrote about them, the kings of this time in south-east England are the first British rulers whose names we know. Among the contemporaries or near-contemporaries of Cassivellaunus were Commius, king of the Atrebates tribe of Hampshire, and Togidubnus (formerly Cogidubnus), king of the Regnenses tribe (Sussex), who built himself the splendid Roman palace at Fishbourne, near Chichester.

Left: In a scene from the Norman Bayeux Tapestry (1082), Harold Godwine is crowned King of England by Archbishop Stigand.

TRIBAL AND ROMAN RULE
TO AD449

When Roman general and dictator Julius Caesar invaded Britain from Gaul in 54BC, he encountered organized resistance under the command of Cassivellaunus, king of the Catuvellauni tribe, which occupied the territory of modern Hertfordshire. Cassivellaunus was probably the most powerful man in Celtic Britain at that time, but he was not the chosen leader of a united country. His tribal state was one of several in fierce competition: rivals in

Above: One of the coins issued in the name of Tasciovanus. His principal mint was at St Albans, the Catuvellauni capital.

what would become south-east England included the tribes of the Regnenses (occupying Sussex), the Cantiaci (Kent), the Atrebates (Hampshire) and the Trinovantes (Essex).

Caesar, who famously declared, '*Veni, vidi, vici*' ('I came, I saw, I conquered'), in fact had mixed success on his two invasion raids of Britain in 55BC and 54BC. But, on the second raid, Cassivellunus was unable to prevent his opponent from returning to Gaul with alliance agreements and hostages.

Almost everything we know about British rulers of this period comes from Roman written sources. Cassivellaunus is the first British native whose name is recorded, because Caesar wrote it down. However, coinage also provides some evidence. For example, Cassivellaunus's successor as ruler of the Catuvellauni, Tasciovanus, is the first British ruler whose face and name can be seen on a coin, which was minted *c.*10BC.

The next king of the Catuvellauni, Cunobelinus (ruled AD10–41) was described as *Rex Britannorum* ('King of

Above: Julius Caesar led two seaborne invasions of Britain in 55–54BC. Both times he landed on Deal Beach in Kent.

the Britons') by the Roman historian Suetonius, but like his predecessor Cassivellaunus he was by no means the ruler of a united land, merely the most important and powerful of several rival kings. Nevertheless, he called himself *rex* and after conquering the Essex territories of the Trinovantes ruled almost the whole of south-east England from his capital at Colchester.

INVASIONS FROM ROME

Roman emperor Claudius launched a new invasion of Britain in AD43, landing an army of 40,000–50,000 well-organized troops on the coast of Kent. Many tribes, mindful of the benefits of Roman trading links as well as the might of the invading army, accepted rule from Rome under a consular governor of Britain. The first was Aulus Plautius, who governed until AD47.

Some Britons put up resistance. Cunobelinus died in AD40, to be replaced by his sons Caratacus and Togodumnus, who both chose to fight the Romans. Togodumnus was slain in combat and Caratacus was driven to the west until AD50 when, after a defeat at

---

KING LEAR

One of the legendary British kings recorded by Geoffrey of Monmouth is King Leir, whose story, known from British and Irish folklore, was used by William Shakespeare as the basis for his great tragedy *King Lear*.

Geoffrey of Monmouth recounted that Leir ruled for 60 years and that, in the course of his reign, he founded the city of Leicester. Monmouth's narrative was reworked by 16th-century chronicler Raphael Holinshed, who wrote that Lear governed Britain for around 40 years *c.*800BC. Holinshed was one of William Shakespeare's key sources for *King Lear*.

The tale of Lear was also told by Edmund Spenser in his allegorical epic *The Faerie Queene*. According to the legend, the king in his old age unwisely divided his country between his daughters on the basis of their professions of love for him. The most devoted daughter, Cordelia, refused to make profession of her love on demand, so the king cut her off from her inheritance and split the kingdom between his harsh elder daughters Goneril and Regan. They mistreated him and he lost his wits.

In the version told by Monmouth, Leir is reunited with Cordelia and comes back to the throne, but in Shakespeare's better-known version, Cordelia dies and Lear grieves for her with words of devastating simplicity.

the hands of Plautius's successor as Roman governor, Ostorius Scapula, he fled to Yorkshire. There Cartimandua, queen of the Brigantes and an ally of Rome, handed Caratacus over to the invaders. Caratacus and his family were transported to Italy. He famously made such a dignified appeal for mercy that Emperor Claudius allowed the British king and his family to live on in Rome.

ANGER OF A ROYAL WIDOW

The year AD60 saw the death of Prasutagus, king of the Iceni tribe of Norfolk. As a client king under Roman rule, he left half his estate to the Emperor Nero and half to his two daughters, but imperial officials disregarded these instructions and attempted to seize the entire inheritance, while Roman soldiers ran amok, flogging Prasutagus's widow, Boudicca and raping her daughters.

Boudicca and the Iceni rose in revolt, slaughtering as many as 70,000 Romans and their allies. However, at Mancetter (Warwickshire) her 100,000-strong army was humiliated by a Roman force barely one-tenth its size. Boudicca took poison rather than be captured.

Below: Togidubnus, king of the Regnenses tribe of Sussex, accepted Roman rule. He built a splendid palace at Fishbourne.

The occupying Roman army made steady progress in stamping out pockets of Celtic-British resistance. In the years AD77–84, Roman governor Julius Agricola won major victories in southern Scotland, northern England and Wales, more or less completing the process, although parts of Wales and northern England remained resistant and a large portion of Scotland was never incorporated into the empire. The conquest initiated over 300 years of Roman rule in Britain, when the kings of rival British states were subject to a

Above: Warrior queen. This 1902 statue celebrates Boudicca's heroic resistance against Roman tyranny. It stands by the Houses of Parliament in central London.

consular governor appointed by Rome. However, in about AD410 the Britons effectively declared independence, expelling the Roman administration. Initially the patterns of Roman life in Britain carried on. As time passed and the Romans did not return, there was increasing competition between Celtic rulers and Romanized Britons, as well as waves of invasion by Germanic peoples from the east, Irish from the west and Picts from the north.

A British ruler named Vortigern ('Great king') was pre-eminent by *c.*AD430. To bolster defences against the northern Picts, he hired Germanic mercenaries and rewarded them by allowing them to settle along the eastern coast of Britain.

In AD449, however, settlers led by Horsa ('Horse') and Hengest ('Stallion') began to seize land and operate independently. The scene was set for centuries of struggle between Germanic incomers and British natives, whom the incomers tended to call 'Welsh' (meaning, in this instance, 'foreigners').

ARTHUR
KING OF CAMELOT

In folklore, legend and literature, King Arthur of Camelot, lord of the Knights of the Round Table, is revered above all other kings and queens. Narratives of the golden age of chivalry in his court at Camelot are tinged with knowledge of its inevitable decay and self-destruction, an elegiac sadness rooted in the knowledge that all things – youth, physical perfection, political achievement, life itself – must pass.

THE HISTORICAL ARTHUR

Stirring legends of King Arthur grew up around the life of a relatively minor 5th- or 6th-century British or Welsh prince who fought against the advancing Saxons and who was perhaps the British leader at a famous victory over the Saxons at 'Mount Badon' c.AD500. Arthur was first mentioned by name in the *Historia Brittonum* ('History of the Britons') by the Welsh cleric Nennius c.AD830, some 300-odd years after his probable death. Nennius lists 12 battles in which Arthur took on the Saxons, including the great triumph at Mons Badonicus (Mount Badon). In the slightly later *Annales Cambriae* ('Annals of Wales', c.AD960) the anonymous chronicler records that Arthur led his people to victory at Mount Badon in AD516 but was killed in battle at 'Camlann' in AD539.

An earlier reference by the British priest Gildas in his *De excidio et conquestu Britanniae* ('The Ruin and Conquest of Britain', c.AD550) describes an

Above: Arthur and his queen Guinevere leave a banquet, from a manuscript by French poet Chrétien de Troyes (d.1183).

unnamed British war leader who triumphed at the Battle of Mount Badon (here dated to c.AD500) and who was probably Ambrosius Aurelianus, the historical prototype for Arthur. One theory contends that the name Arthur, which means 'bear man', was a nickname given to Ambrosius by his men because he was big and hairy like a bear or because he wore the bearskin cloak of late Roman officers.

Many historians locate Mount Badon near Bath in southern England, perhaps at the vast hillfort of Little Solsbury Hill, which archaeologists have shown was used by the British at the end of the 4th century. They suggest that Arthur's victory there drove back West Saxons advancing from the Thames Valley. However, other clues point to the north of England and some believe that 'Camlann' might refer to Birdoswald (Cumbria), which was known as Camboglanna in the Roman era.

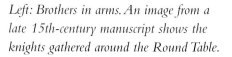

Left: Brothers in arms. An image from a late 15th-century manuscript shows the knights gathered around the Round Table.

If Arthur was active in that region in the early 6th century, then he cannot have been combating Saxons, for their advance had not reached this area.

But the search for the historical Arthur is probably beside the point: the King of Camelot is mainly a figure of legend, whose enduring importance lies in his use by successive ages as a symbol of a past golden age of knightly virtue, right government and peace.

THE LEGEND GROWS

In Welsh folklore and early literature King Arthur began to be associated with tales of wonder and magic. The 12th-century Welsh prose romance *Kulhwch and Olwen* identified Arthur with a band of heroes, an idea that would develop into the Arthurian court and the Knights of the Round Table. The legend was given life by Geoffrey of Monmouth in his *Historia regum Britanniae* ('History of the Kings of Britain', *c.*1135–9). His version contains many familiar elements: the magician Merlin changes Uther Pendragon, King of Britain, into the likeness of Gorloise, Duke of Cornwall, so Uther can sleep with Gorloise's ravishing wife, Ygerna. Arthur is born as a result of this union, and crowned king at a time when the

Below: The 'Arthurian' round table in the Great Hall of Winchester Castle was made in the 1270s, in Edward I's reign.

KING ARTHUR'S INFLUENCE AND LEGACY

The romance of Arthur's court at Camelot and of the company of the Knights of the Round Table, together with the popularity of the Continental tradition of courtly love, inspired the enduring cult of chivalry at the royal courts of England in the 14th–16th centuries. King Edward III and his leading barons were devoted to the practice of jousting and in 1348 Edward founded the knightly Order of the Garter based on that of Arthur and the Knights of the Round Table, whom he regarded as historical figures. At the Tudor courts of King Henry VIII and Queen Elizabeth I, the Arthurian chivalric tradition was still in full flower: Edmund Spenser used Malory's *Le Morte d'Arthur* as a key source for his poem in praise of Elizabeth, *The Faerie Queene* (*c.*1590).

The Arthurian tradition became very popular once more in the Victorian period, when the Pre-Raphaelite artistic movement used Arthurian themes in painting, stained glass and other forms, while English poet Alfred, Lord Tennyson wrote *The Idylls of the King* (1842) using elements of the legend.

In the 20th century, the narrative of King Arthur was the inspiration for the English novelist T.H. White's series of books *The Once and Future King*, which in turn inspired the Broadway musical *Camelot* (1960). In the English language, the word Camelot has come to be used to describe any golden age doomed to end before its time, such as the administration of US President John F. Kennedy, which was cut short by his assassination in Dallas, Texas, in 1963.

---

country is threatened by marauding Saxons. He trounces the Saxons, then defeats the Irish and Picts, marries Guinevere and inaugurates a golden age of chivalry. When he travels to France to defeat a Roman army, he leaves England in the care of his nephew Mordred, who seduces Guinevere and usurps the throne. Upon his return, Arthur is defeated and killed in Cornwall.

Geoffrey of Monmouth's work was translated into French in the *Roman de Brut* (1155) of the Anglo-Norman author Wace. The *Roman* was the first book to mention the round table used at Arthur's court. A group of 13th-century French romances known to scholars as the 'Vulgate' and 'post-Vulgate' cycles then developed the elements of the legend: an illicit romance between Arthur's queen, Guinevere, and his knight, Lancelot; the quest for the Holy Grail and the identification of Lancelot's son, Sir Galahad, as the only knight pure enough to succeed in the Grail quest. Another strand of the Vulgate cycle developed the theme of Arthur's childhood and the

narrative of how he proved his royal standing by drawing the magic sword Excalibur from stone. The legend of King Arthur had a new flowering in England in the 15th and 16th centuries, with Monmouth's *Historia* and Sir Thomas Malory's English prose romance, *Le Morte d'Arthur* (*c.*1470).

Below: The Arthurian legend developed in a series of French romances. This image is from a 15th-century Grail manuscript.

ANGLO-SAXON KINGDOMS
AD500–871

Waves of Germanic invaders swept into Britain in the 5th and 6th centuries AD. There were three main groups: the Angles, from the region of Angulus (modern Angeln district) in northern Germany on the Baltic coast; the Saxons, from the North Sea Coast between the Jutland peninsula and the River Weser; and the Jutes, probably from Jutland in Scandinavia. The Angles settled mainly in East Anglia and to the north of the river Humber, and gave their name both to England and the English language; the Saxons settled largely in southern England; and the Jutes made their home in Kent.

They spread out across south-east England, meeting only the occasional setback. Among the most notable of these was at Mount Badon, the heroic British victory *c.* AD500 celebrated in the mythology of King Arthur. By *c.*AD600, seven main Anglo-Saxon kingdoms were established: Mercia, Northumbria, East Anglia, Kent, Wessex, Sussex and Essex. The British Celts held only Wales and the south-western kingdom of Dumnonia, part of today's Somerset, Devon and Cornwall.

Below: This helmet was among the treasure buried with a king – probably Raedwald of East Anglia – at Sutton Hoo c.AD625.

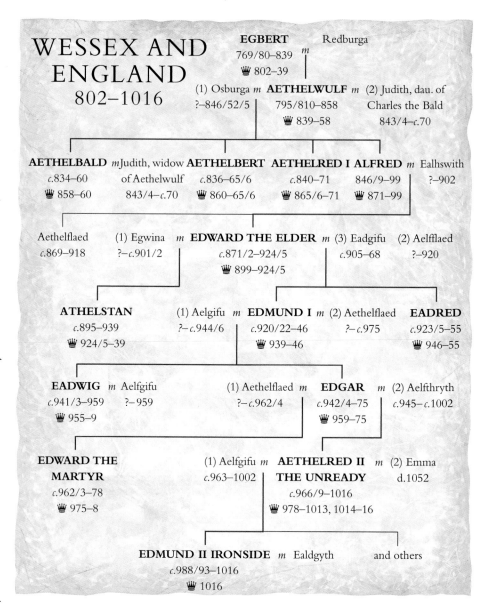

WESSEX AND ENGLAND 802–1016

- **EGBERT** 769/80–839 ♛ 802–39 *m* Redburga
  - (1) Osburga *m* **AETHELWULF** *m* (2) Judith, dau. of Charles the Bald — ?–846/52/5 | 795/810–858 ♛ 839–58 | 843/4–*c.*70
    - **AETHELBALD** *c.*834–60 ♛ 858–60 *m* Judith, widow of Aethelwulf 843/4–*c.*70
    - **AETHELBERT** *c.*836–65/6 ♛ 860–65/6
    - **AETHELRED I** *c.*840–71 ♛ 865/6–71
    - **ALFRED** 846/9–99 ♛ 871–99 *m* Ealhswith ?–902
      - Aethelflaed *c.*869–918
      - (1) Egwina ?–*c.*901/2 *m* **EDWARD THE ELDER** *c.*871/2–924/5 ♛ 899–924/5 *m* (3) Eadgifu *c.*905–68 | (2) Aelfflaed ?–920
        - **ATHELSTAN** *c.*895–939 ♛ 924/5–39
        - (1) Aelgifu ?–*c.*944/6 *m* **EDMUND I** *c.*920/22–46 ♛ 939–46 *m* (2) Aethelflaed ?–*c.*975
        - **EADRED** *c.*923/5–55 ♛ 946–55
          - **EADWIG** *c.*941/3–959 ♛ 955–9 *m* Aelfgifu ?–959
          - (1) Aethelflaed ?–*c.*962/4 *m* **EDGAR** *c.*942/4–75 ♛ 959–75 *m* (2) Aelfthryth *c.*945–*c.*1002
            - **EDWARD THE MARTYR** *c.*962/3–78 ♛ 975–8
            - (1) Aelfgifu *c.*963–1002 *m* **AETHELRED II THE UNREADY** *c.*966/9–1016 ♛ 978–1013, 1014–16 *m* (2) Emma d.1052
              - **EDMUND II IRONSIDE** *c.*988/93–1016 ♛ 1016 *m* Ealdgyth — and others

KINGDOMS IN COMPETITION

The rival Anglo-Saxon realms were drawn into competition, seeking territory and wider control. Northumbria and Mercia were the dominant forces in the 7th century. Northumbria began the century as two kingdoms, those of Bernicia and Deira. These were combined by AD616.

Under Edwin (AD616–33), Oswy (AD642–70) and Ecgfrith (AD670–85), Northumbria became a power to be reckoned with, especially after Oswy defeated and killed his rival warrior-king, Penda, ruler of Mercia in AD655. Northumbria's importance began to

Below: An illuminated manuscript of the first words of Saint Luke's Gospel, from the Lindisfarne Gospels, written c.AD694.

Right: Kings of Kent. Aethelbert (left) was the first Christian Anglo-Saxon king and Eadbald (right) was his successor.

decline after Ecgfrith was killed fighting the Picts at Nechtansmere near modern Forfar on 20 May AD685.

In Mercia, King Wulfhere (AD657–70) expanded southwards as far as the River Thames. The Mercian ruler Aethelbald (AD716–57) called himself 'King of Britain' and seized London and the whole of modern Middlesex from Essex, as well taking control of large parts of Wessex and even conquering territories in Wales. However, he was assassinated by his bodyguard in AD757. His successor was the renowned Offa, who declared himself 'King of the English' and ruled most of Wessex, and all of Sussex, Kent and East Anglia as well as his Mercian heartland. His fame spread far and wide and he was addressed as 'brother' by great Charlemagne, King of the Franks, when negotiating trade terms. Offa also embarked upon the building of a vast – but not continuous – earth barrier along Mercia's border with Wales – Long sections of 'Offa's Dyke', a vast construction, 149 miles (240km) long, 11ft (3.3m) tall and 22 yards (20m) in width, still stand today.

After Offa's death in AD796, Wessex rose to become the pre-eminent Anglo-Saxon kingdom under the rule of King Egbert. Egbert annexed Sussex, Kent and Essex and also campaigned to the west, taking control of former Celtic lands in modern Devon and Cornwall. To the north, he defeated the Mercians in AD825 at the Battle of Ellendun

From the late 8th century, all Anglo-Saxon kings faced a common foe, the marauding Vikings, whose first raid on England was at Portland in Wessex c.AD786. Egbert of Wessex defeated a Cornish and Viking army in AD838 at Hingston Down, Cornwall, but the raiders remained a major problem for Anglo-Saxon England until the reign of Egbert's grandson, Alfred the Great.

THE RISE OF CHRISTIANITY

Aethelbert, the long-lived King of Kent (r. AD560–616), was the first Anglo-Saxon monarch to adopt Christianity. Under the influence of his Frankish queen, who had already been baptized in the religion, Aethelbert allowed a Christian missionary from Rome, Augustine, to settle and begin preaching at Canterbury. Augustine, who was hugely influential and who won many converts, was made the first Archbishop of Canterbury. In AD600 King Aethelbert himself converted to Christianity.

Further north, Christian missionaries spreading south from Scotland were disseminating a distinct form of Christianity that followed Irish instead of Roman customs. Christianity had been established in Ireland since as early as c.AD400–450. The Irish monk Saint Colomba founded a monastery on the island of Iona off the west coasts of Scotland in c.AD563 and Saint Aidan came from Iona to found the celebrated monastery of Lindisfarne, off the coast of Northumberland in northern England, in AD634. It was here that the beautifully illuminated Lindisfarne Gospels were made in about the year AD694.

By this date, the Roman Christian tradition had won an important victory over its Irish counterpart on the mainland. This was decided at the Synod of Whitby called by King Oswy of Northumbria in AD663–4.

KINGS OF IRELAND

From time immemorial, according to the songs of the Celtic bards, Ireland was governed by a high king, who ruled from Tara (north of modern Dublin). In the bardic tradition, the first high king was Niall Noígiallachi ('Niall, Taker of Nine Hostages'), who led military campaigns into Britain.

In fact, the Ireland they described consisted of more than 100 clan groupings (*tuatha*), each with an elected king. *Tuatha* were clustered in larger regional groups, each under one king acting as overlord. The main groups were the Cuig Cuigi ('Five Fifths'), Connacht (Connaught), Laighin (Leinster), Midhe (Meath), Mumhain (Munster) and Ulaidh (Ulster). The historical Niall was a king of Midhe (d. early 5th century). His descendants, ruling from Tara, were claiming to be kings of all Ireland by the 6th century. From AD795, all the Irish kingdoms faced an onslaught from the invading Norse Vikings, who founded the settlement that would become Dublin in AD841. The kings of Mumhain, ruling from Cashel, grew powerful enough to sack the Norse settlements at Limerick and Dublin. The acclaimed Brian Boru, ruler of Mumhain, became the first true high king of all Ireland in 1002.

ALFRED THE GREAT

AD871–899

As Alfred came to the throne of Wessex, aged 22 in AD871, his kingdom and, indeed, the whole of Anglo-Saxon England, was seemingly at the mercy of Viking invaders. Nonetheless, he managed to contain and then drive back the Viking threat and to rule with wisdom and energy for almost three decades. In his reign, learning was revived in England and the incomparable *Anglo-Saxon Chronicle* begun. He is the only monarch in English history to have been awarded the epithet 'Great'.

THE VIKING ONSLAUGHT

After the landing of a Danish Viking 'Great Army' in East Anglia in AD865, the Vikings had taken York, captured

Below: The Great King Alfred. Hamo Thorneycroft's statue of Alfred was unveiled in Winchester in 1901.

Northumbria in AD867 and taken control of East Anglia in AD869. However, in the spring of AD871, Alfred and his brother King Aethelred of Wessex led the men of Wessex in a morale-boosting victory over the Vikings on the Ridgeway at Ashdown in Berkshire, killing thousands of invaders, including five earls and a king.

A few weeks later, on 23 April AD871, Alfred came to the throne on Aethelred's death, but the Ridgeway victory brought little lasting benefit to the new king. Almost at once Alfred's army was scattered far and wide by a renewed Viking assault that hit when he was attending Aethelred's funeral at Wimborne. One of Alfred's first acts as king, therefore, was to 'buy peace' by bribing the Vikings. This brought respite for a few years, while the Vikings were occupied in conquering Mercia, but in

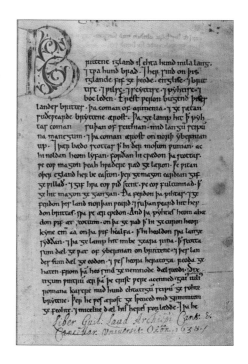

Above: The Anglo-Saxon Chronicle was unusual for the period in being written entirely in Anglo-Saxon rather than Latin.

KING ALFRED THE GREAT, AD871–899

Born: c.AD849, Wantage
Father: King Aethelwulf of Wessex
Mother: Queen Osburga
Accession: 23 April AD871, Dorset
Queen: Ealhswith (m. AD868; d. AD905)
Succeeded by: His son, Edward 'the Elder'
Greatest achievement: Containing the Viking threat
AD871: Leads English army to victory over Vikings at Ashdown
May AD878: Defeats Vikings at Battle of Edington
c.AD886: Captures formerly Mercian city of London
c.AD887: Learns Latin and begins translation of Pope Gregory the Great's *Cura Pastoralis* ('Pastoral Care or Rule')
Death: 26 Oct AD899, Winchester

AD877 a Viking force led by Guthrum renewed the attack and captured Exeter. The following January, when a surprise attack on Chippenham resulted in another Viking victory, Guthrum won control of most of Wessex.

Alfred was forced to retreat deep into the Somerset countryside and, from a base at Athelney in the Somerset marshes, he began to conduct a guerrilla war against the invaders. In May AD878, he led an army of men from Wiltshire, Somerset and Hampshire in a famous victory over the Vikings at Edington, at the northern limit of Salisbury Plain, and drove the remnants of the enemy all the way back to their base at Chippenham, a distance of over 15 miles (24km).

Under the peace treaty that followed, the Vikings agreed to withdraw entirely from Wessex and Guthrum accepted baptism as a Christian. Alfred showed great generosity to his former adversary, recognizing him as an adoptive son.

THE KING WHO BURNT THE CAKES

At the lowest ebb of his reign, while King Alfred was forced to live incognito in deepest Somerset, he was scolded by a swineherd's wife. The story goes that Alfred was seated by the fireside in the swineherd's hut, lost in thought as he tried to plot a way of defeating the seemingly invincible Vikings. Perhaps he did not hear the woman of the house, who was leaving for a few moments, ask him to mind the cakes that she was baking, or perhaps he forgot to do as he was asked. When she returned and found that the cakes were burnt she was furious and battered the king about the head with her stick. This apocryphal story can be

Right: Sir David Wilkie painted King Alfred burning the cakes in 1806.

traced as far back as a *Life of St Neot*, written in the 10th century, and was mistakenly included in the edition of Bishop Asser's *Life of King Alfred* (AD893) which was published by Archbishop Matthew Parker in 1574. Thereafter it appeared in many modern accounts of Alfred's life and the story continues to be told into the 21st century.

THE DANELAW

Guthrum and the Vikings pledged not to attack Wessex, but they remained in strength in other English kingdoms, establishing themselves in East Anglia and the lands to the north and east of Watling Street, the Roman road running from London in the south-east to Chester in the north-west. Here, in the 'Danelaw' (roughly modern Yorkshire, east Midlands and East Anglia), they flourished, establishing several prosperous settlements.

Alfred meanwhile set about strengthening the military defences of Wessex. He built several *burhs*, or fortified towns, reorganized the army so that half could be rested while the other half was on campaign and created an English navy, consisting of manoeuvrable warships of his own design, each with 60 oars. The navy proved its worth in AD896 by defeating a powerful Danish Viking raiding party off the Isle of Wight.

THE REVIVAL OF LEARNING

Alfred was able to provide stability for the people of Wessex and, in a previously lawless era, his kingdom came to be known for its just royal laws and honest administration. He collected laws from diverse sources and published an English law code. His coins recognized him as *Rex Anglorum* ('King of all the English') and he was increasingly accepted as king of all Englishmen and women not subject to the Danes.

As a young child, Alfred had visited the learned Frankish court, which had been established early in the 9th century by the great Charlemagne. This experience may have inspired him to initiate and oversee the revival of education and learning that occurred at his court in Winchester and throughout his kingdom.

Alfred himself was illiterate until his later teens but he determined that free-born English boys should have the chance to learn through reading, and established schools to this end. He also saw that those books in his words 'most necessary for all men to know' should be made available to his people in their own tongue and provided for their translation.

King Alfred learned Latin at the age of 38 in order to translate the *Cura Pastoralis* ('Pastoral Care or Rule') by Pope Gregory the Great, and he subsequently sent a copy of his translation with an exquisite aestel (bookmark) to every bishop in the kingdom. A key part of his commitment to knowledge was his sponsorship of the vast *Anglo-Saxon Chronicle,* an historical record of England which went as far back as the Roman invasion.

A TEMPLATE FOR KINGSHIP

Alfred was plagued throughout his life by illness. Some scholars suggest he was an epileptic, others that he suffered from haemorrhoids or from venereal disease contracted in his bachelor days before his AD868 marriage to Ealhswith of Mercia. Yet despite the debilitating effect of his illness, the king brought energy, intelligence, and courage to all his endeavours. He was, in the words of his devoted and perspicacious biographer Bishop Asser of Sherborne, an 'immovable pillar of the people of the west, a just man, an energetic warrior, full of learning in speech, above all instructed in divine knowledge'.

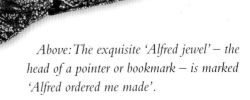

Above: The exquisite 'Alfred jewel' – the head of a pointer or bookmark – is marked 'Alfred ordered me made'.

THE HOUSE OF WESSEX
AD899–978

The great King Alfred was succeeded in AD899 by his son, Edward, who performed wonders in consolidating and extending his father's achievements. Where Alfred had concentrated on defence against the Viking threat, Edward took an aggressive approach. In a series of stunning victories in AD917, he captured Essex and the East Midlands and forced the Vikings of East Anglia to submit to the rule of Wessex. Then, in AD918, he further expanded the kingdom by taking control of western (English) Mercia from its female ruler, his niece Aelfwynn, and conquered Danish Mercia (the region known as 'the Five Boroughs') and the Danish-ruled kingdom of East Anglia. Before his death, on 17 July AD924, he had also received the

Below: King Edgar, one of the first kings to be anointed with holy oil, with St Dunstan, creator of the coronation ceremony.

submission of the rulers of the Welsh kingdoms of Dyfed and Gwynnedd, while the kings of the northern Danish territory of York and the independent Anglo-Saxon earldom of Northumbria, Strathclyde and Alba (Scotland) had accepted him as 'lord'. His dominance extended across the entire island.

LINE OF SUCCESSION
Edward, usually known as 'the Elder', was briefly succeeded by his son Aelfweard, (who ruled for just 16 days and may have been assassinated) and then by another son, Athelstan, who won further victories for Wessex and was the first king to rule all of England.

Athelstan was succeeded by another of Edward's sons, Edmund I (AD939–46), who suffered a major setback when Olaf Gothfrithson, King of the Dublin Norse, captured York and parts of Mercia in AD940. Edmund won back most of the land for Wessex in

ATHELSTAN, KING OF ENGLAND, AD924–939
Birth: *c*.AD895
Father: Edward the Elder
Mother: Egwina
Accession: 17 July AD924
Coronation: 4 Sept AD924
Succeeded by: His half-brother, Edmund I
Death: 27 Oct AD939, Gloucester

AD942, then died an untimely death four years later, aged just 25, when he was killed in a skirmish while attempting to defend his steward from a thief named Leofa.

Yet another son of Edward the Elder, Eadred (AD946–55), defeated Erik Bloodaxe, the last Viking king of York, in AD954 and consolidated the Wessex dynasty's control of all England. His natural death at around the age of 30 created something of a succession crisis, as his two sons were just 15 and 14.

ROYAL SEX SCANDAL
The accession of Edmund's elder son Eadwig threatened all that Alfred's heirs had achieved, for Eadwig, while a good-looking young boy, lacked the seriousness his position demanded.

His reign began in scandal when he left his coronation feast and was discovered by the venerable Abbot Dunstan *in flagrante* with both a maiden named Aelfgifu and her mother.

Within two years the kingdom split when Mercia and Northumbria rejected the young king's dubious authority and chose his 14-year-old brother Edgar in his place. Fortunately for the future of England, the dissolute Eadwig died before his 20th birthday, on 1 October AD959, and the energetic, pious and astute Edgar came to the throne in his place.

Right: The lands ruled by Athelstan, King of Wessex. His power reached as far north as York and as far west as Cornwall.

THE LORD'S ANOINTED

Edgar brought to England an era of peace and reform of the kind attributed to his great predecessor Alfred. With his Archbishop of Canterbury, the renowned Dunstan, he introduced church and monastic reforms and developed the idea of the king as God's representative on Earth.

On Whit Sunday, 11 May AD973, Edgar was crowned king of England in a splendid ceremony in Bath that included an anointing: a deliberate reference to the ordination of a priest. The coronation-anointing took place 14 years into the reign because by AD973 Edgar was 30, the minimum age for a priest. Later the same year, in a celebration at Chester, Edgar was recognized as overlord by no fewer than eight kings – including King Kenneth II of Scots, King Malcolm of Strathclyde and King Iago of Gwynnedd.

ATHELSTAN: KING OF ALL ENGLAND

Edward the Elder's son Athelstan (AD934–9) was the first king to rule all of England. In AD927 he pushed Wessex's borders further north by conquering the Viking kingdom of York. He received vows of submission from the Britons of Cornwall and five kings in Wales c.AD930. The *Anglo-Saxon Chronicle* praised him in ringing tones: 'Royal Athelstan, lord of warriors, giver of rings to men, with his kingly brother Edmund, won glory beyond compare with their sharp swords.'

Athelstan was the king who first sent Englishmen into military action on the European Continent. In AD939 he despatched a fleet to Flanders to back his nephew, Louis of France. He commissioned an illuminated edition of Bede's *Life of St Cuthbert* that contains a portrait of the king. This is the first contemporary image in English history of a ruling monarch.

Left: Athelstan's portrait is contained by a capital G in an illuminated edition of Bede's Life of St Cuthbert.

Edgar was a great reformer. He oversaw a realignment of county boundaries that would endure for more then 1000 years (until 1974), and also reformed weights and measures and the coinage, introducing a new currency in AD973.

Below: Athelstan's coins were inscribed 'King of all Britain', indicating that the Scots and Welsh accepted his authority.

FROM AETHELRED II TO HARTHACNUT

AD978–1042

The rule of Aethelred II (AD978–1016) began in treachery. He came to the throne at the age of just 10, when his half-brother King Edward was stabbed to death by Aethelred's retainers.

King Edward was the son of King Edgar by his beautiful first wife, Aethelflaed, while Aethelred was Edgar's son by his second wife, Aelfthryth. Naturally, Aelfthryth was opposed to Edward's accession and when the king was killed during a visit to Aelfthryth's house, suspicion inevitably fell upon her. Although no proof was ever found of the involvement of Aethelred or of Aelfthryth in the murder, the deed cast a shadow over the king's rule.

AN INHERITANCE LOST

Aethelred's reign ended with the king sidelined and his son Edmund 'Ironside' facing defeat in the struggle against Cnut's Danish forces. In just 38 years, Aethelred lost a stable and prosperous kingdom, which had been built up over 100 years by Alfred the Great and his heirs.

The king is often known as 'King Aethelred the Unready'. This derives from 'Aethelred unraed', which is a pun on his name and means 'Noble advice, evil advice'. In fact, Aethelred's reign was not a failure because he was 'unready' or unprepared, or because he took poor advice – although he did make a number of costly mistakes that had profound long-term effects. The principal reason Aethelred lost a kingdom was the sudden surge of Danish power under King Harold Bluetooth and his son Sweyn in the years after AD980.

It certainly did not help that Aethelred was an unconvincing general. He lost much of the support of his leading subjects in a series of defeats by the Danish invaders. After the Battle of Maldon, in Essex, in AD991, Aethelred initiated a doomed policy of bribing the Danes to stay away with vast sums of gold and silver. Over a period of 20 years, these bribes, known as *Danegeld*, cost England a fortune. Aethelred made

Above: Aethelred, Rex Anglorum ('King of the English'). In his reign, a few of these pennies would have bought a sheep.

another decision with damaging long-term consequences when, in 1001, he married Emma, daughter of the Duke of Normandy, as part of an Anglo-Norman alliance designed to outmanoeuvre the Danes.

Aethelred then made plans for a massacre of all the Danes in England on St Brice's Day, 13 November 1002, However, this was only partially carried out and served to provoke the Danes into fiercer military action. In 1013 King Aethelred fled to Normandy, and the Danish king, Sweyn, claimed the English throne. However, Aethelred returned the following year and succeeded in ousting Sweyn's son, Cnut. To win the support of his leading nobles he was forced to pledge reforms and surer government in future in the first such agreement between monarch and subjects in English history.

In 1015 Aethelred's son Edmund – known as 'Ironside' for his strength and courage – revolted against his father's rule and took control of the army. Aethelred died, powerless, in April 1016 and after a bruising series of battles Edmund Ironside and Cnut agreed to share power, with Edmund taking Wessex and Cnut ruling all the land to the north of the River Thames.

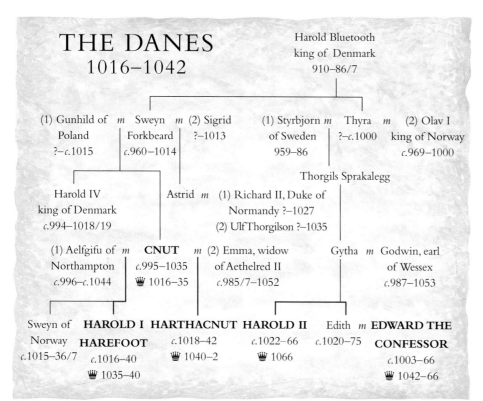

THE DANES 1016–1042

Harold Bluetooth king of Denmark 910–86/7

(1) Gunhild of Poland ?–c.1015 *m* Sweyn Forkbeard c.960–1014 *m* (2) Sigrid ?–1013

(1) Styrbjorn of Sweden 959–86 *m* Thyra ?–c.1000 *m* (2) Olav I king of Norway c.969–1000

Harold IV king of Denmark c.994–1018/19

Astrid *m* (1) Richard II, Duke of Normandy ?–1027
(2) Ulf Thorgilson ?–1035

Thorgils Sprakalegg

(1) Aelfgifu of Northampton c.996–c.1044 *m* **CNUT** c.995–1035 ♔ 1016–35 *m* (2) Emma, widow of Aethelred II c.985/7–1052

Gytha *m* Godwin, earl of Wessex c.987–1053

Sweyn of Norway c.1015–36/7

HAROLD I HAREFOOT c.1016–40 ♔ 1035–40

HARTHACNUT c.1018–42 ♔ 1040–2

HAROLD II c.1022–66 ♔ 1066

Edith c.1020–75 *m* **EDWARD THE CONFESSOR** c.1003–66 ♔ 1042–66

Above: The scandal that dogged Aethelred. A 15th-century manuscript depicts events surrounding the murder of King Edward.

CNUT RULES ALONE

When King Edmund Ironside also died, on 30 November 1016, his subjects in Wessex were left to the mercy of King Cnut. The new king acted swiftly to secure his position: he had Edmund Ironside's brother, Eadwig, killed; he executed the powerful earls of East Anglia and Mercia; and he married King Aethelred's widow, Emma of Normandy, hoping to consolidate his standing in the country by marrying its queen.

Cnut already had two sons by his existing English wife, Aelfgifu, but under the terms of the new marriage agreement, only his children by Emma would have a claim to the throne. In 1019 Cnut became King of Denmark

THE KING WHO COULD NOT TAME THE WAVES

The best-known story about King Cnut is the legend – of doubtful authenticity – that he taught his flattering courtiers a lesson by pretending he thought he could tell the waves to go back. With an empire including land on both sides of the North Sea, Cnut was the most powerful ruler in Europe in the early 11th century.

As an increasingly devout Christian Cnut was ever mindful of the divine power from which his own claim to rule was derived. Impatient with courtiers who flattered and praised him too much, he played along with the idea that he thought he was important enough to command the waves. He had a throne placed on the edge of the beach and ordered the waves to retreat. When they did not, and indeed rushed over his feet

Right: Cnut and his queen, Emma, present a cross to the New Minster, Winchester, in an image of c.1030.

and drenched his robes, he pretended to be angry and ordered them back once more. When he finally dropped the game, he told his courtiers never again to forget the extent to which his own mortal power was limited and bade them to remember how little consequence it had beside the power of God, who could command the oceans.

and at a stroke England became part of a Scandinavian empire. Cnut was increasingly committed to imperial expansion in Norway and wanted to maintain England as a secure, untroublesome source of wealth. Cnut

was a Christian and made pilgrimages to Rome in 1027 and 1031. According to a chronicler of the 12th century, Cnut changed from a wild warrior to 'a most Christian king'.

A TROUBLED SUCCESSION

Cnut had proved himself a very effective ruler. However, after his death in 1035, his dynasty was destroyed by infighting in just seven years. Cnut's designated successor was Harthacnut, but because he was in Norway at the time of Cnut's death, Harthacnut appointed his half-brother Harold regent. Harold then claimed the throne but he was soon dead, probably having been assassinated. Harthacnut returned to England to occupy the throne, but he died on 8 June 1042, apparently from overindulging in drink at a wedding.

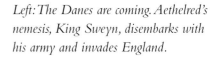

Left: The Danes are coming. Aethelred's nemesis, King Sweyn, disembarks with his army and invades England.

EDWARD THE CONFESSOR AND HAROLD II

1042–1066

On the death of Harthacnut, the throne passed to Edward, son of Queen Emma by her first husband, Aethelred. His accession was manoeuvred by the ruthless Earl Harold Godwine. In 1045 Edward married Godwine's daughter, Edith. Then, in 1051, Edward attempted to assert his independence by exiling Godwine and by naming his cousin, Duke William of Normandy, as his successor – if William's later account is to be believed. Nevertheless, the following year Godwine returned stronger than ever to win the full support of the king's ruling council, the Witan. Godwine died in 1053 but his sons, Tostig, Gyrth and Harold, occupied powerful positions as the earls of Northumbria, East Anglia and Wessex.

STRUGGLE FOR SUCCESSION

In his final years, Edward was much occupied with rebuilding the abbey church of St Peter at Westminster. By

Below: Edward the Confessor celebrates Easter at a banquet in 1053. Godwine's death is depicted in the foregound.

EDWARD THE CONFESSOR, KING OF ENGLAND, 1042–1066

Birth: *c.*1003, Islip
Father: Aethelred II
Mother: Emma of Normandy
Accession: 8 June 1042
Coronation: 3 April 1043, Winchester Cathedral
Succeeded by: Harold II
Death: 5 Jan 1066, Westminster

---

the time it was consecrated, in December 1065, however, he was too ill to attend, and on 5 January 1066 he died. Harold Godwineson, Earl of Wessex, was crowned King of England the very next day, claiming to have been designated by Edward as his successor.

William of Normandy was enraged. He claimed both that Edward had chosen him as successor in 1051 and that Harold Godwine had pledged to support William's claim on a mission to Normandy in 1064. William also had a hereditary claim to the throne, albeit

---

HAROLD II, KING OF ENGLAND, 1066

Birth: *c.*1022
Father: Godwine, Earl of Wessex
Accession: 5 Jan 1066
Coronation: 6 Jan 1066, Westminster Abbey
Succeeded by: William I
Greatest achievement: Securing the throne, Battle of Stamford Bridge
Jan 1066: Marries Ealdgyth, sister of Earls of Mercia and Northumbria
25 Sept 1066: Defeats Harald Hardrada and Earl Tostig at the Battle of Stamford Bridge
14 Oct 1066: Defeated by Duke William of Normandy at the Battle of Hastings; dies during battle

---

a tenuous one: he was the great-nephew of King Cnut's second wife, Emma of Normandy. In addition to William, King Harold faced two other rivals for his throne: King Harald Hardrada of Norway and Edgar the Atheling (or 'prince'). Harald's claim to the throne was inherited from his nephew King Magnus the Good of Norway who had acquired the claim by treaty from Harthacnut in 1036. Edgar the Atheling had the most convincing hereditary claim as Aethelred II's great-grandson, but he was fatally handicapped by being just 14 years old and having no proof that he was a man of war or fit for power.

King Harold had the throne by virtue of acting swiftly. His two rivals prepared to invade. In addition, Harold had made an enemy of his brother, Earl Tostig, by depriving him of power in Northumbria because of his incompetence, and replacing him with the earl of Mercia's brother, Morcar.

In the summer of 1066 Harold waited for the twin invasions – but nothing happened. In September he

allowed his soldiers to return home, but then had hastily to gather an army and march north to York when news reached him that Earl Tostig and King Harald Hardrada had mounted a joint invasion. He routed their combined force at the Battle of Stamford Bridge, near York, on 25 September.

Harold now heard that William had landed a fleet 250 miles (400km) to the south. He gathered his 7000-odd troops and marched south in 11 days. He could have chosen to hold back and engage the Norman army in the course of the winter, but instead staked everything on a quick victory in battle at Hastings.

Right: The Norman cavalry take on Anglo-Saxon foot soldiers in a Bayeux Tapestry scene from the Battle of Hastings.

THE BATTLE OF HASTINGS

The battle near Hastings on 14 October 1066 lasted all day. King Harold's army of 7000, including many untrained peasants, occupied a strong position on high ground, with Duke William's smaller force of around 4000 – consisting of archers, foot soldiers and cavalry – arranged on the slope beneath them.

The Normans opened the assault with their archers and the Anglo-Saxons fought back with spears and slings. When the Norman cavalry attacked, its men and horses were cut to pieces by Harold's soldiers with their double-handed axes. Twice the Norman cavalry pretended to retreat, drawing groups of Anglo-Saxons from the high ground, and then turned to destroy them.

At one point, scholars believe, William's horse was cut from under him and the word went among his men that he was dead. However, he claimed another horse and, once in the saddle, raised his helmet to rally his troops by showing them his face, declaring, 'Look, I am alive – and by God's grace will still win the victory!'

The decisive moment in the battle came when King Harold was killed. From the evidence of the Bayeux Tapestry (made about 1077) he was either shot in the eye with an arrow or had his legs hacked from under him by a Norman foot soldier. The Anglo-Saxons fought on without a leader, but at dusk they broke and fled, leaving the field to Duke William of Normandy. Some historians believe that King Harold's corpse was chopped into many pieces by victors maddened by battle.

Left: A 13th-century manuscript depicts the moment of Harold's death.

After his triumph over Harold at Hastings, William marched his Norman army across south-east England in a show of military might. Canterbury and Winchester surrendered almost immediately and by December resistance was over and the throne was secured.

Below: Feudal power. An enthroned William I grants lands to Alain de Brittany, who swears loyalty in return.

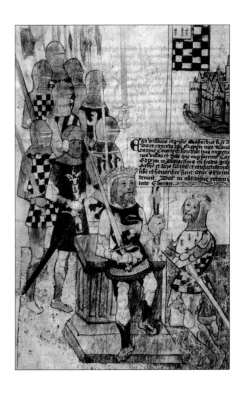

WILLIAM I THE CONQUEROR
1066–1087

 The illegitimate Norman known in his homeland as Guillaume le Bâtard was crowned King William I of England in Edward the Confessor's abbey church at Westminster by Ealdred, Archbishop of York, on Christmas Day, 1066.

His initial victory had been won by military might and it was consolidated with great ruthlessness in the ensuing six years in the face of a series of revolts. William and his army put down rebellions in Cornwall in 1068 and then repeated uprisings in the north in 1068–9, during which Norman earl Robert de Comines was burnt alive with 900 men in Durham. King Sweyn II of Denmark and Edgar the Atheling captured York briefly during this period, burning the Minster. William's brutal reprisals laid waste the countryside so that thousands of people died of starvation and disease. In 1070, Anglo-Saxon rebels in East Anglia led by Hereward the Wake joined up with Danish sailors to plunder Peterborough Abbey. William made peace with King Sweyn II in June 1070 and the Danes departed, but Hereward became a focus for Anglo-Saxon rebels who gathered to him in his hideout on the Isle of Ely. William defeated them in April 1071, but Hereward escaped to carry on the fight as an outlaw.

INVASION CONSOLIDATED
Across the country the Normans raised imposing castles to keep their peace. In 1067–8 alone, William built castles in Exeter, Warwick, Nottingham, York, Lincoln, Huntingdon and Cambridge. In the course of his reign, William raised 78 castles, including the White Tower, now the heart of the Tower of London, and the New Castle near the mouth of the river Tyne that gave its name to Newcastle. In the Welsh Marches, on

Above: A scene from the Bayeux Tapestry depicts William the Conqueror with Bishop Odo and Robert de Mortain.

the English border with Wales, William settled powerful Norman nobles who were allowed free rein so long as they kept the Welsh and English under control.

The Normans now 'invaded' the land-owning aristocracy and the Church, replacing Anglo-Saxons in a host of key positions. In 1066 there were 4,000 landowning *thegns* in King Harold's country, but by 1087 (the year of William's death) this territory had been appropriated and shared out among 200 French aristocrats; only two Anglo-Saxon landowners remained.

William made his intentions towards the Church clear in 1070, when he replaced the native Archbishop of Canterbury, Stigand, with his own man, Lanfranc, previously Abbot of St Stephen's in Caen, Normandy. Most of the country's bishops and abbots were replaced by Norman clerics.

By about 1072, England was securely conquered. William spent most of the remainder of his reign in France, campaigning against the French king, Philip I, the Counts of Flanders and Anjou and, from time to time, against his own eldest son, Robert Curthose.

THE DANES AND DOMESDAY
William returned to England in 1085, to face a threatened Danish invasion under King Cnut IV. To raise finance for an army he declared a land tax on all, but then – realizing the need for more accurate records of landholdings – he commissioned a land survey, 'The Description of All England', dubbed *The Domesday Book* by his subjects because there was no escaping it, just like the Day of Judgement. This remarkable survey was completed in less than a year and presented to William on 1 August 1086. In the end, King Cnut died and the invasion did not come.

William then returned to France, where he died in 1087 after being seriously injured in a fall from his horse during an attack on Nantes as part of a campaign against Philip I. He was buried on 12 September in St Stephen's Abbey, Caen. His unfortunate mourners left the building gagging after the king's fat and decomposing body burst its sarcophagus, emitting a stench of rotting flesh.

Before he died, William was ill for some weeks and had time to repent. He reputedly confessed his brutality with some remorse, saying, 'I am stained with the rivers of blood that I have spilled'.

WILLIAM I THE CONQUEROR, KING OF ENGLAND, 1066–1087
Birth: *c.*1027, Falaise, Normandy
Father: Robert, Duke of Normandy
Mother: Herleva
Accession: 14 Oct 1066
Coronation: 25 Dec 1066, Westminster Abbey
Queen: Matilda, daughter of Baldwin V (m. *c.* 1050–2; d. 2 Nov 1083)
Succeeded by: His son William II Rufus
Death: 9 Sept 1087, Priory of St Gervais, Rouen

WILLIAM II RUFUS
1087–1100

On his deathbed, William I is supposed to have left the English crown to his second son, William, while giving Normandy to his eldest son, Robert Curthose, and giving his third son, Henry, no land but the compensation of £5,000. William secured the crown for himself before Robert could act. Travelling swiftly to England from Normandy, he was crowned king in Westminster Abbey on 26 September 1087.

Before a year was out, William faced rebellion. His uncle, Bishop Odo, Earl of Kent, led an uprising with the aim of replacing William with Robert. Although the rebels captured several towns, the rebellion collapsed, Odo and his supporters were exiled and William seized their land.

William spent some years fighting on and off in Normandy to seize his brother's lands and reunite their father's inheritance. In 1096 Robert Curthose joined the First Crusade and, to finance his part in the expedition, pawned his duchy to William for 10,000 marks. Before Robert returned from the Crusade, William was dead – perhaps assassinated – after what was officially a hunting accident in the New Forest.

WILLIAM II RUFUS, KING OF ENGLAND, 1087–1100

Birth: c.1056/60, Normandy
Father: William I
Mother: Matilda of Flanders
Accession: 9 Sept 1087
Coronation: 26 Sept 1087, Westminster Abbey
Succeeded by: His brother, Henry I
Death: 2 Aug 1100, New Forest, Hampshire

Left: William II's red hair, which won him the nickname 'Rufus' (from Latin for red), is not visible in this later portrait.

ROYAL WHODUNIT

King William II died in suspicious circumstances while out hunting in August 1100. The official story is that the king and his friends were taking their pleasure in the New Forest, Hampshire, the vast 95,000-acre hunting preserve created by William I, when the fateful arrow was loosed by William's friend, Walter Tirel. The arrow struck William in the chest and he died at once. However, suspicion is inevitable that William's brother Henry, who was in the party and who subsequently became king, was somehow involved in the 'accident'. Henry rode at once to Winchester, where he secured the royal treasury, then proceeded to London to have himself elected king by the ruling council.

Crucially, the 'accident' happened while the rightful heir, Duke Robert Curthose of Normandy, was away on the First Crusade and Tirel himself was never punished.

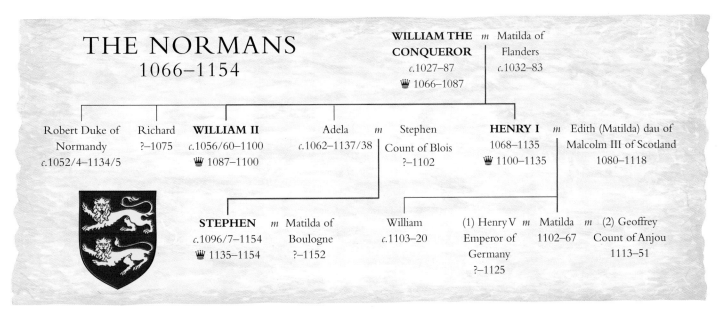

THE NORMANS
1066–1154

	WILLIAM THE CONQUEROR c.1027–87 ♛ 1066–1087	*m*	Matilda of Flanders c.1032–83

Robert Duke of Normandy c.1052/4–1134/5	Richard ?–1075	**WILLIAM II** c.1056/60–1100 ♛ 1087–1100	Adela c.1062–1137/38	*m* Stephen Count of Blois ?–1102	**HENRY I** 1068–1135 ♛ 1100–1135	*m* Edith (Matilda) dau of Malcolm III of Scotland 1080–1118

STEPHEN c.1096/7–1154 ♛ 1135–1154	*m* Matilda of Boulogne ?–1152	William c.1103–20	(1) Henry V Emperor of Germany ?–1125	*m* Matilda 1102–67	*m* (2) Geoffrey Count of Anjou 1113–51

HENRY I
1100–1135

The first years of King Henry I's reign were clouded by doubt over his succession and by revolts led by barons seeking to put Duke Robert Curthose of Normandy, William the Conqueror's eldest son, on the throne. These were effectively ended by Henry's defeat of Robert at Tinchebrai, Normandy, in September 1106.

The new king also bolstered his position by recalling and making peace with Anselm, the Archbishop of Canterbury, with whom William II had quarrelled bitterly. Anselm had been in exile overseas since 1097, but returned early in the new reign, at Henry's invitation, in October 1100.

A NEW MORALITY

One of the main points of disagreement between William II and Archbishop Anselm had been the Archbishop's disapproval of what he saw as decadence at William's court. In a Lenten sermon in 1094, Anselm had attacked effeminacy and the practice of homosexuality at the court, denouncing the men of the court for growing beards, wearing their hair long and sporting extravagant shoes.

Life at Henry's court was far more sober and clean-shaven, and Henry was a loyal patron of the church. For example, he sponsored the rebuilding of Canterbury Cathedral choir, a project that was completed in 1130.

Henry's marriage to Edith, the great-granddaughter of Edmund II 'Ironside' (who was briefly king in 1016) and sister of King Edgar of Scots, cemented a valuable alliance with the Scots and allowed Henry to reinforce his claim to the throne by marrying into the royal line of the Anglo-Saxons. After the wedding, Edith took the Norman name Matilda, perhaps in honour of Henry's mother.

LOSS OF THE WHITE SHIP

In 1120, Henry I won a diplomatic triumph by agreeing a peace treaty with King Louis VI of France, under which the long-disputed duchy of Normandy was to pass to Henry's only legitimate male heir, his son Prince William the Atheling, on Henry's death. However, as the royal court returned to England from Normandy, a ship transporting Prince William, sank in the Channel. Apparently the pilot was drunk and he had allowed the vessel, the White Ship, to run on to a rock off Barfleur. Everyone on board died, apart from one Rouen butcher.

NO MALE HEIR

Although Henry had fathered 21 children, only two of them were legitimate. The White Ship tragedy killed William the Atheling, his only legitimate male heir, leaving only a daughter, Matilda, who in 1114 had married Holy Roman Emperor Henry V. On 1 January 1127 Henry prevailed over his reluctant barons, persuading them to accept Matilda, by now a widow, as his heir. But baronial opposition to her succession only grew stronger when, the following year, she married Count Geoffrey of Anjou, who was nicknamed

Left: A detail from a manuscript image of the loss of the White Ship shows Henry mourning the death of his sons.

Above: Henry's jester, Rahere, founded the priory church of St Bartholomew the Great in Smithfield, London, in 1123.

'Plantagenet' because he used the broom plant (Latin: *planta genista*) as his family emblem.

King Henry I died in December 1135 after overindulging in eating lampreys. Although his daughter Matilda was his official heir, many barons instead supported the claim of Henry's nephew Count Stephen of Blois.

HENRY I, KING OF ENGLAND, 1100–1135

Birth: Sept 1068, Selby, Yorkshire
Father: William I
Mother: Matilda of Flanders
Accession 3 Aug 1100
Coronation: 5/6 Aug 1100, Westminster Abbey
Queens: (1) Matilda, daughter of Malcolm III of Scotland (m. 11 Nov 1100; d. 1 May 1118); (2) Adeliza, daughter of Geoffrey VII, Count of Louvain (m. 1121; d. 1151)
Succeeded by: His nephew, Stephen of Blois, although Henry had named his daughter Matilda as his successor
Death: 1/2 Dec 1135, near Rouen, Normandy

STEPHEN
1135–1154

On learning of his uncle King Henry I's death, Count Stephen sailed to England and was crowned in Westminster Abbey on 26 December 1135. His accession, in direct contravention of the oath he and leading English barons had sworn to King Henry I to support the Empress Matilda as Queen, plunged the country into a bitter civil war.

YEARS OF CIVIL TURMOIL

In 1139, the Empress Matilda and her husband Geoffrey of Anjou, in alliance with her half-brother, the illegitimate Robert, Earl of Gloucester, landed an army in south-west England to claim the throne and set up their own royal court in Bristol. In 1140 Earl Ranulf of Chester rose in revolt and captured Lincoln. In 1141, King Stephen was defeated by Robert, Earl of Gloucester, at the battle of Lincoln, on 2 February.

Right: The coronation of King Stephen, a miniature from the Flores Historiarum *by the Benedictine monk and chronicler Matthew Paris (d. 1259).*

STEPHEN, 1135–1154

Birth: *c.*1096/7 (before 1100), Blois, France

Father: Stephen Henry, Count Palatine of Blois, Brie, Chartres and Meaux

Mother: Adela of Normandy

Accession: Usurps the throne 22 December 1135

Coronation: 26 Dec 1135, Westminster Abbey

Queen: Matilda (m. before 1125; d. 2/3 May 1152)

Succeeded by: His second cousin, Henry II

Death: 25 Oct 1154, Dover, Kent

He was imprisoned in chains in Gloucester's castle. The Empress Matilda was elected Queen at Winchester on 8 April. Stephen's wife – another Matilda – arrived with an army of mercenaries from Flanders.

When the armies of the two Matildas met at Winchester, the troops of the Empress were defeated and her key ally Gloucester was taken prisoner. The Empress Matilda's brief ascendancy was over; she was forced to exchange Stephen for Gloucester, and Stephen was crowned King of England for a second time, at Canterbury on Christmas Day 1141.

The civil war ran on for another decade or more. The key years were 1147–8, when the Earl of Gloucester died, and 1153 when Stephen lost his only heir with the death of his beloved son Eustace. However, the bruising conflict could not truly be said to be over until, on 6 November 1153, in the Treaty of Wallingford, King Stephen agreed that the Empress Matilda's son Henry Plantagenet was to be his heir and would inherit the throne. The following year, on 25 October 1154, King Stephen died and Henry inherited the throne of England as King Henry II.

CHAPTER TWO

THE PLANTAGENETS

1154–1399

When Henry, Duke of Normandy, Count of Anjou, Touraine and Maine and Duke of Aquitaine was crowned King Henry II of England in 1154, he founded England's longest-reigning dynasty, that of the Plantagenets. The House of Plantagenet ruled for 331 years, until 1485, supplying 14 English kings.

The name 'Plantagenet' came from a nickname for Henry II's father, Geoffrey, Count of Anjou. The nickname derived from *planta genista*, the Latin name for the broom plant, and was applied to Geoffrey either because he used the plant as his emblem, because he wore broom sprigs in his hat or because he planted broom on his land to provide cover when hunting. Although historians use the name Plantagenet, Count Geoffrey's descendants went without any form of surname for 250-odd years.

Some historians identify the first kings of the Plantagenet line – Henry II, Richard I and John – as 'Angevins', from their title as Count of Anjou, and reserve the title 'Plantagenet' for the succeeding kings, Edward I, Edward II and Edward III. The three Plantagenet kings who were descendants of the Duke of Lancaster are identified as the House of Lancaster (Henry IV, Henry V and Henry VI), and the final three, descendants of the Duke of York, as the House of York (Edward IV, Edward V and Richard III). Nonetheless, all were Plantagenets.

Left: In 1382, Richard II married Anne of Bohemia at Westminster. Both were aged 15. The illustration is from the Chronicles of Jean Froissart *(c. 1333-1400).*

HENRY II
1154–1189

At Christmas 1154 the newly crowned Henry II celebrated the first undisputed accession to the English throne since that of Harold II in 1066. Henry's claim to the throne was not beyond dispute: it was as the son of Empress Matilda, who had plagued Stephen I's reign with repeated assertions of her own royal pedigree as the daughter of King Henry I. However, he acceded peacefully under the terms of an 1153 agreement between Stephen and Matilda that guaranteed the crown for Matilda's son. After years of civil war in Stephen's reign, there was no appetite for a struggle against the king among the nobles and people of England.

FIRST PLANTAGENET KING

In England, Henry acted swiftly and decisively to quell opposition among the barons, destroying a number of castles that had been used as bases for

HENRY II, KING OF ENGLAND, 1154–1189:	
Birth: 5 March 1133, Le Mans	**June 1162:** Thomas à Becket appointed Archbishop of Canterbury
Father: Geoffrey Plantagenet, Count of Anjou	**1163:** Overlord of Wales
Mother: Empress Matilda, daughter of King Henry I of England	**1166:** Assize of Clarendon establishes trial by jury
Accession: 25 Oct 1154	**29 Dec 1170:** Becket killed, Canterbury
Coronation: 19 Dec 1154, Westminster Abbey	**1174:** Overlord of Scotland under Treaty of Falaise
Queen: Eleanor of Aquitaine (m. 1152; d. 1204)	**12 July 1174:** Henry does penance in Canterbury Cathedral
Succeeded by: His son, Richard I	**1175:** Overlord of Ireland under Treaty of Windsor
Greatest achievement: Founding Royal House of Plantagenet	**Death:** 6 July 1189, Chinon, France

tyrannical local rule. He also made a series of legal reforms that created the foundation of the English 'common law' that has endured for centuries. To replace the existing local courts presided over by the barons, he established royal courts with the king's officials travelling on a circuit to bring impartial justice to all parts of the realm. The law was codified in works such as the *Treatise on the Laws and Customs of England*, written by the king's justiciar, or legal officer, Ranulph Glanville. Trial by a 12-man jury was introduced in 1166.

Henry, the first Plantagenet king and ruler over western Europe's largest 'empire', was king of England by sovereign right. He held all of his French titles and lands – as Duke of Normandy, Count of Anjou, Touraine and Maine and Duke of Aquitaine – as a vassal of the king of France, and herein lies one of the causes of the Hundred Years War.

HENRY AND BECKET

For the first ten years of the reign, Henry and Thomas à Becket, England's leading prelate, were close allies: Henry appointed Becket Chancellor in one of his first acts as king in January 1155, and in June 1162 named Becket Archbishop

of Canterbury. However, in 1164 the pair argued after Becket rejected the Constitutions of Clarendon, which attempted to establish royal authority over churchmen and prevent clerics appealing on legal matters to the Pope in Rome.

Becket fled to a Cistercian monastery in France and Henry confiscated the Archbishop's English possessions. By 1170 Henry and Becket had moved towards reconciliation and, at the king's invitation, Becket returned to England. Once there, however, he defied Henry once more by suspending or excommunicating bishops who had opposed him. In a moment of exasperated rage, Henry is reported to have cried out, 'Will no one rid me of this turbulent priest?' This was the trigger for the attack that led to Becket's death. Four knights, led by Sir Reginald FitzUrse, confronted Becket in Canterbury Cathedral and violated its sanctuary by killing him with their swords.

Within 18 months and amid outrage, the Pope declared Becket a saint. Papal legates found that Henry was not responsible for the murder, and the king made a public act of penance at Becket's tomb in Canterbury Cathedral in July 1174.

Above: King and Archbishop in dispute. A manuscript of 1300 depicts Henry and Becket engaged in an intense debate.

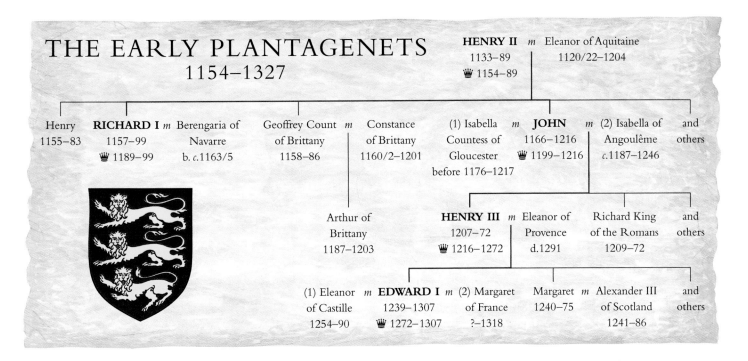

THE EARLY PLANTAGENETS
1154–1327

			HENRY II *m* Eleanor of Aquitaine	
			1133–89 · 1120/22–1204	
			♛ 1154–89	

| Henry 1155–83 | **RICHARD I** *m* Berengaria of 1157–99 · Navarre ♛ 1189–99 · b. *c.*1163/5 | Geoffrey Count *m* Constance of Brittany · of Brittany 1158–86 · 1160/2–1201 | (1) Isabella *m* **JOHN** *m* (2) Isabella of Countess of · 1166–1216 · Angoulême Gloucester · ♛ 1199–1216 · *c.*1187–1246 before 1176–1217 | and others |

Arthur of Brittany 1187–1203

HENRY III *m* Eleanor of 1207–72 · Provence ♛ 1216–1272 · d.1291

Richard King of the Romans 1209–72

and others

(1) Eleanor *m* **EDWARD I** *m* (2) Margaret of Castille · 1239–1307 · of France 1254–90 · ♛ 1272–1307 · ?–1318

Margaret *m* Alexander III 1240–75 · of Scotland 1241–86

and others

A FORBIDDING QUEEN: ELEANOR OF AQUITAINE

Henry's queen, Eleanor of Aquitaine, was the most powerful woman of her age, who married two kings and was the mother of two more. She encouraged her sons to revolt against their father and, according to tradition, arranged the slaughter of King Henry's beloved mistress, Rosamund Clifford.

Eleanor was the wife of King Louis VII of France before she married Henry. Just eight weeks before Eleanor wed Henry, in the summer of 1152, Louis had had their marriage annulled by mutual consent. Although she was 12 years older than the 18-year-old Henry and was capricious in character, she was a great beauty and became a patron of the arts, especially of courtly literature. She brought with her the vast territories of Aquitaine in central-southern France,

which she had inherited from her father and which, under feudal law, reverted to her on her divorce.

Henry and Eleanor had seven children, including two future kings of England: Richard I and King John. However, king and queen grew apart and an ageing Eleanor was increasingly jealous of King Henry's many younger mistresses. In 1173 she encouraged a rebellion by her sons and even tried to join the campaign, disguised as a man, but was captured by King Henry's troops. Henry survived this revolt but a second family rebellion in 1189 sent him to his deathbed.

After 1173 Henry and Eleanor were publicly estranged and the king lived with his favourite mistress, Rosamund Clifford. According to legend, Eleanor killed 'Fair Rosamund' – in one account, confronting her with a dagger and a cup of poison and forcing her to choose which way to die. She outlasted her husband and lived to see two of her sons on the throne. She died, aged 82, in 1204.

Left: After the failed rebellion of 1173, Eleanor was captured by her husband; a fresco of c.1200 from Chinon, France.

Without shirt or shoes, he walked to the cathedral and flung himself before the tomb of his former enemy and friend before submitting to a penitential flogging at the hands of monks.

ROYAL OVERLORD

In a series of treaties, Henry won recognition as feudal overlord from rulers at home and abroad. In 1163 Owain Gwynedd, king of Gwynedd, reaffirmed Henry's overlordship. Henry had power over Scotland under the Treaty of Falaise signed in 1174 with King William of Scots, and he was overlord of Ireland under the 1175 Treaty of Windsor.

FAMILY BETRAYAL

Although Henry crushed a revolt by his sons and estranged queen in 1173, he was outmanoeuvred and defeated 16 years later by his son Prince Richard in alliance with King Philip II of France. Henry was forced to pay homage to Philip for all England's territories in France and to pass England and his Plantagenet holdings to Richard. It is said that when the ageing king discovered that his favourite youngest son, John, had joined the alliance against him, it broke his heart and two days later he died. His final words were, 'Shame, shame on a vanquished king'.

RICHARD I THE LIONHEART
1189–1199

King Richard I is celebrated as the English warrior-king above all others, dubbed *Coeur de Lion* ('Lion Heart') for his chivalrous achievements on the Third Crusade (1190–92) and on the battlefields of Europe. In fact, he had limited connection to his English territories and only spent six months of his 10-year reign in England.

Above: Crusader king. The English Luttrell psalter (1340s) depicts Richard fighting his great foe, Saladin, on crusade.

KNIGHTLY AMBITION

Born in 1157 in Oxford, Richard was raised in France where his French mother, Queen Eleanor of Aquitaine, held court at Poitiers. He was schooled in the arts of knighthood and grew up with a passionate desire to prove himself a chivalric prince in the Holy Land, perhaps inspired by tales of his fearless mother's travels there during the Second Crusade (1147–49) when she was still married to her first husband Louis VII of France. Encouraged by Eleanor, Richard joined a revolt against his father King Henry II in 1173, when he was only 15 years old. In 1179 he proved himself in battle, capturing the castle of Taillebourg during a campaign in Aquitaine to put down rebel lords. At his coronation on 3 September 1189 he cut a dashing figure. Tall, blue-eyed, he was the perfect knight.

Below: In an image from the Chronicles of England *(c. 1470) of Jean de Wavrin, Richard processes to his coronation.*

IN THE MIDDLE EAST

Richard's main interest at the start of his reign was to raise money for a new crusade. To this end, in December 1189, he cancelled the Treaty of Falaise, under which the Scots recognized English overlordship, in return for a payment from King William of Scots of 10,000 marks. He departed for the Holy Land with Philip of France in the following year. However, the venture got off to a bad start because the kings quarreled before they even reached the Holy

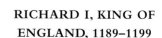

RICHARD I, KING OF ENGLAND, 1189–1199

Birth: 8 Sept 1157, Oxford
Father: King Henry II of England
Mother: Queen Eleanor of Aquitaine
Accession: 6 July 1189
Coronation: 3 Sept 1189, Westminster Abbey; recrowned 17 April 1194, Winchester
Queen: Berengaria of Navarre (m. 1191; d. 1230)
Succeeded by: His brother, John
Greatest achievement: Military victories on Third Crusade
Dec 1189: Cancels Treaty of Falaise
1191: Captures Arsuf in Holy Land
1192: Imprisoned by Holy Roman Emperor Henry VI
1193: Freed on payment of ransom of 150,000 marks
Death: 6 April 1199, Châlus, France

Above: Richard is shown imprisoned in Vienna (left) and in the moment before being shot by a crossbowman at Châlus.

Land. At a stop in Sicily, Philip and Richard argued over Richard's refusal to keep his promise to make a dynastic marriage with Philip's sister, Alice.

Philip travelled ahead. Richard captured Cyprus after a quarrel with its Greek king and there, on 12 May 1191, he married Berengaria of Navarre, who was crowned Queen of England. In the Holy Land, Richard and Philip patched up their quarrel and together captured Acre. Here Richard quarrelled bitterly with Duke Leopold of Austria over the sharing out of the gains and also alienated Philip once more.

Philip left for home in August 1191, while Richard proceeded to capture Arsuf and to march on Jerusalem. He twice came within view of the holy city but was forced to retreat because of the strength of Saladin's defending army. The crusade ended in a truce, under which Saladin remained in control of

Jerusalem, but Christian pilgrims were permitted to visit the city. Richard set sail for home in September 1192. Although he had not achieved all his goals, his victories re-established a viable Crusader kingdom in the Holy Land.

TROUBLE AT HOME

Richard had laid plans to protect his English realm while he was away. He entrusted William Longchamps, Bishop of Ely, with the position of Chief Justiciar and the power to rule the country, while making his brother Prince John promise not to travel to England from France or attempt to take control there. The plan failed. John did not keep his word and set up his own government, driving Longchamps into exile in France and plotting with Philip of France to prevent Richard returning.

CAPTURED IN AUSTRIA

Hearing of this plot while returning from the Holy Land, Richard attempted to evade capture. After he was shipwrecked he disguised himself but he

was recognized in Vienna and imprisoned, first by his enemy Duke Leopold of Austria and then by the Holy Roman Emperor Henry VI. His release was made subject to payment of a king's ransom of 150,000 marks, the equivalent of 35 tonnes of gold.

In England, the new Chief Justiciar Hubert Walter somehow managed to raise this vast sum. Freed in 1193, Richard returned to England the following year and was crowned for a second time by Walter, now Archbishop of Canterbury, at Winchester on 17 April 1194. The king forgave his brother for his part in the plot against him. Then, after spending a mere two months in England he returned to France to seek revenge against Philip and to fight for the return of lost territories. He died there on 6 April 1199 after the wound made in his shoulder by a crossbow bolt at Châlus became gangrenous. He was buried alongside his father – and later joined by his mother, Eleanor of Aquitaine – at Fontevrault Abbey in Normandy.

Below: Coeur de lion. Richard's image as the crusading king par excellence has inspired artists of many eras.

JOHN
1199–1216

 An unprincipled opportunist, King John made a series of bad decisions in pursuit of short-term advantage. By the end of his reign he had not only lost the vast French empire created by his father, Henry II, but had also alienated the crown's leading English supporters as well as the pope and the Church establishment.

'LACKLAND' AND LOYALTY

John was the youngest of King Henry's sons, and because his older brothers received large territorial inheritances and he was given nothing, he was nick-named 'Lackland'. In 1189 John joined Richard in revolt against their father. This betrayal is said to have left Henry a broken man, for John was his father's favourite. Then when Richard I was on

Right: John's favourite hunting lands were said to be Clipstone in Sherwood Forest, home of legendary outlaw Robin Hood.

**JOHN, KING OF ENGLAND,
1199–1216**

Born: 24 Dec 1167, Oxford
Father: King Henry II of England
Mother: Queen Eleanor of Aquitaine
Accession: 6 April 1199
Coronation: 27 May 1199, Westminster Abbey
Queens: (1) Isabella of Gloucester (m. 1176; divorced 1200; d. 1217); (2) Isabella of Angoulême (m. 1200; d. 1246)
Succeeded by: His son, Henry III
Greatest achievement: Defeat of Irish revolt, 1210
Nov 1209: Excommunicated by Pope Innocent III
1215: Magna Carta
Death: 18 Oct 1216, Newark

---

the Third Crusade in 1190–2, John reneged on a promise not to interfere in England. He declared him-self King of England when Richard was captured and imprisoned in Austria on his way home from the Holy Land in 1192. Richard nonetheless forgave John and the pair fought in tandem to regain Richard's French lands.

On Richard's death in April 1199, John was invested Duke of Normandy in Rouen and then crowned King of England in Westminster Abbey. When John dropped the banner bearing his ducal insignia at the Rouen ceremony, many saw it as a bad omen.

John came to the throne at the age of 32. As he did so, his attention was focused on safeguarding his French lands in the face of a challenge from his nephew, Arthur of Brittany, who claimed Anjou and Touraine.

THE PRINCE OF ALL WALES

Welsh overlord Llewelyn ab Iorwerth, prince of Gwynedd, established himself as ruler without equal in Wales at the end of King John's reign, earning himself the epithet 'the Great'. Hearing of plans for a joint attack on Gwynedd by King John and Gwenwynwyn, lord of the rival Welsh kingdom of Powys, Llewelyn declared Gwenwynwyn guilty of treachery and marched into his lands to annex them. Gwenwynwyn returned from England to defend Powys, but failed, was injured and forced to retreat to Cheshire. Llewelyn's queen was Joan, an illegitimate daughter of King John. After Llewelyn's death, on 11 April 1240 at Aberconway in Gwynedd, a chronicler called him 'Prince of Wales'.

Above: A 1957 memorial marks the spot at Runnymede near Windsor at which John signed the Magna Carta.

FRENCH LOSSES

In the first year of his reign, after divorcing his first wife, Isabella of Gloucester, John married the 12-year-old Isabella of Angoulême, making an enemy of the French baron Hugh de Lusignan, who had been betrothed to Isabella. The de Lusignans owed John allegiance in his role as Count of Aquitaine but they appealed to his feudal overlord, King Philip of France, for justice in the case of the marriage. John refused to appear before the French king to answer the charges, and Philip dispossessed John of all the lands he held in France, on the grounds that John was a 'contumacious vassal' (since he had failed to fulfil his feudal obligation).

The dispute with the de Lusignans and other French nobles led to war in 1202. John was initially successful, capturing Arthur and the de Lusignans at Mirebeau, but when word got out that he had murdered Arthur, Brittany rose against him and John lost the support of the barons in Anjou and Normandy. He retreated to England in 1203 and by 1206 had lost all his French holdings save Aquitaine.

DISPUTE WITH ROME

When the Archbishop of Canterbury, Hubert Walter, died in 1206, John refused to accept Stephen Langton, the man nominated by the pope, as Walter's successor. The dispute led to John's excommunication by Pope Innocent III in 1209. In theory the pope had the power to order John's subjects to depose him and replace their king with a more godly man, but John backed down. He accepted Langton as archbishop in 1213 and then agreed that Ireland and England were fiefs of Rome. At Winchester on 20 July 1213, Archbishop Langton formally absolved John of his excommunication.

JOHN AND MAGNA CARTA

In 1214 John launched an ill-fated attempt to regain his French possessions that ended with the defeat of his German ally, the emperor Otto of Brunswick, at Bouvines. His campaigns had been extremely expensive and John's English subjects were restless under the weight of taxation that he imposed to finance them. In 1215 a revolt by leading barons forced John to agree to a charter of liberties, *Magna Carta* ('Great Charter') at Runnymede to the west of London.

The charter, which was reissued in 1216, 1217, 1225 and 1297, guaranteed the reform of royal abuses of power and turned out to be the first step in

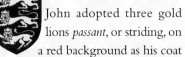

THREE LIONS
John adopted three gold lions *passant*, or striding, on a red background as his coat of arms. He based the device on the emblem used by his father and brother, of two striding lions. Heraldic devices were worn by knights jousting at chivalric tournaments and in battle as an identifying mark. John's three lions were incorporated into the royal seal.

establishing constitutional government in England. It stated that the law had force independently of the will of the king. The following year, when John renounced it, the barons rebelled, imported Louis, the son of King Philip II of France, and prepared to depose John. Before this could happen John died of dysentery at Newark on 18 October 1216. The final event of his reign was a characteristically bungled manoeuvre in which he lost the crown jewels in quicksand while crossing the Wash, a tidal estuary in eastern England.

Below: John's tomb (1232) in Worcester Cathedral is carved with an effigy of the king flanked by St Wulfstan and St Oswald.

HENRY III
1216–1272

Following King John's sudden death and with London in the hands of rebel barons preparing to elevate France's Prince Louis to the English throne, nine-year-old Prince Henry was crowned in great haste at Gloucester Abbey on 28 October 1216. A bracelet belonging to his mother, Queen Isabella, was used in place of the crown because King John had lost the crown jewels. With the Archbishop of Canterbury away in Rome, the ceremony was performed by the French-born Bishop of Winchester.

John's disastrous reign had brought England to its knees and the future of the Angevin dynasty looked grim. However, thanks to an effective regency by William Marshal, Earl of Pembroke, the knight chosen on his deathbed by King John, the country and the dynasty were stabilized. Marshal defeated the rebels in 1217, bringing the civil war to an end, and on his death in 1219 was succeeded by Hubert de Burgh. Henry III took the reins of power in January 1227, aged 20.

ROYAL WEDDING

Henry married the beautiful 19-year-old Eleanor of Provence in Canterbury Cathedral on 14 January 1236. To house

Above: In this miniature of his coronation ceremony, Henry holds a model of Westminster Abbey, rebuilt in his reign.

his new queen in suitable splendour he renovated the royal palace at Westminster, installing glass in the windows and plumbing, fitting large fireplaces and commissioning fine wall-paintings for private chambers. Later the same month, on 30 January 1236, Eleanor was crowned Queen of England, in Westminster Abbey.

The marriage brought trouble, for the influx of the new queen's relatives seeking wealth and power made the English barons resentful. Trouble broke out in the mid-1250s after Henry agreed to provide financial support for Pope Innocent IV's proposed military campaign in Sicily. In June 1258 he was forced to agree to the Provisions of

---

HENRY III, KING OF ENGLAND, 1216–1272

Birth: 1 Oct 1207, Winchester

Father: King John of England

Mother: Queen Isabella of Angoulême

Accession: 18 Oct 1216

Coronations: (1) 28 Oct 1216 Gloucester; (2) 17 May 1220, Westminster Abbey

Queen: Eleanor of Provence (m. 14 Jan 1236; d. 1291)

Succeeded by: His son, Edward I

Jan 1227: Henry takes power at the end of his minority

May 1240: Crowns Dafydd of Gwynedd 'paramount prince in Wales'

June 1258: Provisions of Oxford

1264: Civil war

14 May 1264: Captured by Simon de Montfort

4 Aug 1265: Defeat of Simon de Montfort at Battle of Evesham

Death: 16 Nov 1272, London

KING OF ANIMALS

In London Henry built a menagerie at the Tower of London, partly as a home for the first elephant ever to be brought to England. The beast was a gift to Henry from France's King Louis IX in 1255. It was carried as far as Tilbury Docks by water and then walked the remainder of the way while gaping crowds marvelled at the sight. Earlier, in 1237, Henry had built a leopard house at the Tower, and he was given a polar bear as a gift from the King of Norway in 1252. In keeping a zoo, Henry was following the example of his great grandfather, Henry I, who had kept a collection of camels, lions and leopards at Woodstock in Oxfordshire. Richard I, it is said, even brought a crocodile to England from his travels, but the creature escaped into the Thames.

Oxford, by which a council of 15 barons was created to govern jointly with the king.

DE MONTFORT'S RISE AND FALL

Simon de Montfort, Earl of Leicester, was the driving force behind this challenge to royal authority. Born in France, he had arrived in England in 1229 and set about building a power base. In January 1238 he married the king's sister, Eleanor, thus provoking the anger of

Henry's brother Richard, Earl of Cornwall, and that of leading barons. Exiled as a result in 1239, he won great honour on crusade (1240–2) and during King Henry's unsuccessful invasion of France in 1242. He subsequently became convinced that Henry was unfit to govern, largely because of the king's poor decision-making after sending him to put down a baronial revolt in Gascony in 1248.

In 1264 de Montfort led an open rebellion to reinstate the Provisions of Oxford after they had been repudiated by Henry in 1262 and then annulled at an agreed arbitration by King Louis IX of France. De Montfort defeated the king's army at Lewes in 1264, captured Henry III and his son Edward, and for a year became the effective ruler of England. At this time he called a Parliament that, in addition to barons and clerics, held two burgesses from each borough and two knights from each shire. However, in the summer of 1265, Prince Edward escaped and, joining up with allies, turned on de Montfort and won a crushing victory at the Battle of Evesham in Worcestershire. In death, de Montfort was horribly mutilated by royalist soldiers. His head, hands and feet were cut off and his genitals thrown on to his face.

The king's authority had been restored – by his son. However, de Montfort had achieved a lasting legacy, because England's king would ever afterwards have to be mindful of the will of Parliament.

A PRINCE FOR WALES

In May 1240, amid great ceremony at Gloucester, Henry III crowned Dafydd of Gwynedd the 'paramount prince in Wales'. Dafydd was the younger son of Llywelyn the Great of Gwynedd and his wife Joan, an illegitimate daughter of King John, and was therefore Henry's

Left: Salisbury Cathedral was begun in 1220 and dedicated in 1258. The 404ft (123m) spire was added in 1330.

Above: 14th-century chroniclers stressed Henry's piety. He supported orphans and provided food for paupers. He is even said to have washed and kissed lepers' feet.

nephew. Towards the end of Henry's reign, in 1267, the English king recognised Dafydd's nephew Llywelyn ap Gruffudd as Prince of Wales.

ROYAL PATRON

Henry was a pious and highly cultured man, whose 56-year reign was a golden age of learning, architecture and the arts. In addition to his large-scale renovation of Westminster Palace, Henry oversaw a major rebuilding of Westminster Abbey to house a shrine to the church's original royal founder, Edward the Confessor. The French-trained architect Master Henry de Reyns pulled down all of Edward's church except the nave and rebuilt it in the Gothic style on a French cathedral plan. The work took 36 years and cost £46,000. Henry's reign also saw major work on the magnificent cathedrals at St Alban's, Salisbury, Lincoln and Wells in Somerset. Learning thrived under this cultured king, and the first colleges in Oxford University – Merton, University and Balliol – were founded in the years between 1249 and 1264.

EDWARD I
1272–1307

Edward I came to the throne, aged 33, a proven warrior. He had already fought with distinction in Henry III's campaigns against Welsh prince Llywelyn ap Gruffudd in 1259 and in 1265 had restored royal power by crushing Simon de Montfort's rebellion at the Battle of Evesham. He was in Sicily, returning from fighting on the Eighth Crusade (1270–2) when he was declared king on 17 November 1272.

'LONGSHANKS'

Edward brought a ferocious martial vigour to his reign, forcefully imposing his authority on his realm, ending Welsh independence and waging a series of brutal wars in the north that later earned him the nickname 'Hammer of the Scots'. Standing imperiously 6ft 2in (1.9m) tall – an astonishing height for

---

EDWARD I, KING OF ENGLAND, 1272–1307

Birth: 17 June 1239, Westminster

Father: Henry III of England

Mother: Eleanor of Provence

Accession: 16 Nov 1272

Coronation: 19 Aug 1274, Westminster Abbey

Queens: (1) Eleanor of Castile (m. Oct 1254; d. 1290); (2) Margaret of France (m. 10 Sept 1299; d. 1318)

Succeeded by: His son, Edward II

March 1284: Statute of Rhuddlan

1290: Royal edict expelling Jews from England

1296: Invades Scotland, Battle of Dunbar

1301: Edward's son Edward created first English 'Prince of Wales'

1305: Captures and executes Scottish rebel William Wallace

Death: 7 July 1307 of dysentery at Burgh by Sands, near Carlisle

---

Above: Realm of fortresses. The map shows the network of castles built between 1066 and the end of Edward I's reign in 1307.

the 13th century – he cut a commanding and regal figure and was admiringly known as 'Longshanks'.

At home he carried out much needed legal reforms, improved the efficiency of administration and is remembered as the king in whose reign Parliament's role in government was consolidated. The changes he oversaw in government strengthened rather than diluted royal authority, clarifying Parliament's role as an instrument of the king's rule – used in particular to levy

Above: One of Edward's forbidding Welsh castles, Harlech was built in 1283–90 by his engineer, Master James of St George.

taxes to pay for military campaigns. The legal reforms codified English law, providing a legal basis for inheritance of land and improving public order laws.

VICTORY IN WALES

Llywelyn ap Gruffydd was the first sole ruler of a united Wales. However, he grew overconfident of his position and, when he refused to pay homage to Edward I, provoked a savage 1276 invasion that within a year reduced his realm to a small region in Snowdonia. An uprising led by Llywelyn's brother Dafydd in 1282 provoked a second English invasion in which Llywelyn was killed at Builth and then Dafydd was hung, drawn and quartered as a traitor at Shrewsbury.

Under the Statute of Rhuddlan of March 1284, English officials were brought in to govern the new English-style shires that were to replace the existing Welsh kingdoms. Edward built a series of forbidding castles across Wales at Flint, Rhuddlan, Builth, Conway, Caernarfon, Criccieth, Harlech, Denbigh and Beaumaris to impose his will on what was now a subject country. In Caernarfon castle, in 1284 the king's son Edward was born. Some 17 years later

Below: Liberties confirmed. The 14th-century manuscript, Statutes of England, *shows Edward reissuing Magna Carta.*

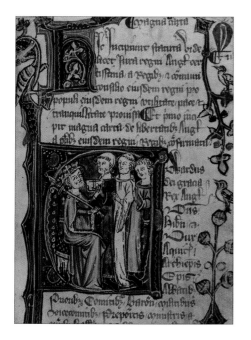

A LOYAL HUSBAND

Henry was devoted to his first wife, Eleanor of Castile. Their marriage in 1254 was a diplomatic one, made when the future king was 15 and his wife just 9, but grew to be a love match. An elegant, dark-haired woman, Eleanor travelled with her husband to Wales, Gascony and even to the Holy Land on crusade. Perhaps their bond was strengthened by a brush with death in 1287, when a lightning strike in Gascony killed two people in the very room in which the royal couple were sitting.

Queen Eleanor bore Edward 11 daughters and 4 sons, including the future Edward II. When she herself died, aged 54, on 28 November 1290, her desolate spouse wrote 'in life I dearly loved her and I will not stop loving her in death'. In her honour he erected 12 Memorial Crosses to mark the places where her funeral cortege stopped on its journey from Harby, in Nottinghamshire, where the queen died, to Westminster Abbey, where she was buried. Three of these crosses survive today – at Geddington and Hardingstone in

Nottinghamshire and Waltham Cross in Essex; a memorial at Charing Cross in London is a 19th-century replica of the original cross that stood there.

Edward married for a second time, on 10 September 1299, again making a diplomatic match when he wed Margaret, the sister of France's King Philip IV. Despite a 40-year age differential between the 60-year-old king and his 20-year-old bride, this marriage too turned out well.

Below: Eleanor's memory was celebrated by this monument at Hardingstone.

this boy, now heir to the throne, was created the first English Prince of Wales. This was the first time an English royal ruler officially took the title of 'prince'.

THE HAMMER OF THE SCOTS

When John Balliol was named King of Scots in 1292 after a two-year interregnum following the death of the infant Queen Margaret, he paid homage to Edward as his feudal overlord. However, in October 1295 the Scots made an alliance with France rather than join Edward in a French military campaign, and the following spring John Balliol refused to pay homage to Edward.

Edward invaded Scotland with a 25,000-strong army and overran Berwick, killing 7,000 of its population, before defeating a Scottish army at Dunbar. King John Balliol abdicated

and, in a humiliating public ceremony, was stripped of his crown and royal finery.

Edward unleashed the force of the English army and its powerful long-bowmen on the Scots again in 1298 and 1300. That year he made a calculated insult to Scottish pride by removing the Scots' ancient coronation stone from its place at Scone and installing it at Westminster as part of a new coronation throne.

Edward invaded Scotland again in 1301–2 and in 1303–5. When he finally captured the outlawed Scottish leader William Wallace, he was taken to London and executed by having his head and limbs severed from his body.

When Edward died near Carlisle, on 7 July 1307, he was travelling north in preparation for yet another of his Scottish campaigns.

EDWARD II
1307–1327

Edward II was blessed with intelligence, bravery and good looks and inherited the throne of a secure and well-governed country. However, he exhibited a self-indulgence and lack of judgement in public and private life that made a bitter enemy of his formidable queen and of prominent barons and that led inexorably to the loss of his crown and a gruesome end in a prison cell.

A ROYAL FAVOURITE

Before he became king, Edward's close friendship – and probably homosexual relationship – with Piers Gaveston, the son of a Gascon knight, caused scandal at court. Edward I is said to have been outraged when his son asked for a gift of territory for his friend. The king exiled Gaveston and reportedly tore at his son's hair, shouting, 'You base-born whoreson! Do you want to give lands

away now, you who have never gained any?' However, there was nothing to stand in Edward's way when he became king and within a month of acceding to the throne he recalled Gaveston and made him Earl of Cornwall, a position normally reserved for the son of the reigning king. Shortly afterwards Edward gave his niece in marriage to Gaveston, then made his friend regent while he, Edward, travelled to France to make a diplomatic wedding match with the French king's daughter, Isabella.

Leading barons led by Thomas, Earl of Lancaster turned against the king, who in 1311 was forced to accede to a series of demands that placed limits on his power and in particular required him to strip Gaveston of his title and send him into exile. Edward did as he was required to do, but Gaveston returned the following year. The angry barons seized the royal favourite and, at Blacklow Hill in Warwickshire, they

Above: Gravity and majesty. Edward II stands between Edwards I and III in a group of statues at York Minster.

Below: Edward II founded Oriel College, Oxford, in 1326 as 'The House of the Blessed Mary the Virgin in Oxford'.

EDWARD II, KING OF ENGLAND, 1307–1327

Birth: 25 April 1284, Caernarfon
Father: Edward I of England
Mother: Eleanor of Castile
Accession: 8 July 1307
Coronation: 25 Feb 1308, Westminster Abbey
Queen: Isabella of France (m. 25 Jan 1308; d. 1358)
Succeeded by: His son, Edward III
Greatest achievement: English economic boom fuelled by exports to continental Europe of English wool
Sept 1311: Ordinances strengthen power of Parliament
24 June 1314: Defeated by Scots in Battle of Bannockburn
1326: Civil war
24 Jan 1327: abdicated
Death: 22 Sept 1327 murdered Berkeley Castle, Gloucestershire

beheaded him. Gaveston's death greatly upset Edward, but had the effect of repairing his relationship with Queen Isabella. The couple's son, who was named Edward after his father, was born on 13 November 1312.

DEFEAT AND HUMILIATION

In 1314, Edward led an English army into Scotland to relieve Stirling Castle, which was besieged by Scottish forces under King Robert I 'the Bruce'. Although they outnumbered the Scots, Edward's army was humiliated in the two-day Battle of Bannockburn, afterwards celebrated as the event that cemented Scottish independence. Edward was forced to flee for his life. In England, Thomas, Earl of Lancaster sidelined the king and established himself as the country's effective ruler.

CIVIL WAR

Edward did not change his ways. He found new favourites in two lords from the Welsh Marches, Hugh le Despenser and his father, also Hugh, to whom he gave an abundance of titles and territories in Wales. Lancaster banished the Despensers in August 1321, and the king went to war on their behalf,

Below: Gothic masterpiece. Edward III honoured his father by building this superb marble tomb in Gloucester Cathedral.

THE DEATH OF KING EDWARD II

After installing Edward III on the throne, Queen Isabella and Roger Mortimer ordered that Edward II be jailed at Berkeley Castle in Gloucestershire and starved to death. But the king, whose spirit must have remained strong, lingered painfully on. The king's minders devised a sadistic means of killing their prisoner that would leave no mark on his body: after a metal funnel was inserted into the king's anus, a red-hot soldering iron was thrust into his bowels. His screams of agony filled the air.

The king's colourful reign and brutal end inspired 16th-century English dramatist Christopher Marlowe to write *Edward II* (*c.*1592), one of the first historical plays of the Elizabethan era. This play in turn inspired the 20th-century filmmaker Derek Jarman to make the acclaimed movie *Edward II* (1991).

Below: Berkeley Castle was built by Roger de Berkeley in the 11th century.

defeating the Earl in the Battle of Boroughbridge, in Yorkshire, in March 1322. Edward then had Lancaster executed, recalled the Despensers and for a short while governed as he pleased. However, trouble was brewing.

Queen Isabella, angered at her husband's relationship with the younger Hugh le Despenser, abandoned him. She began to live openly in France with Roger Mortimer, Earl of March, an exiled opponent of the Despensers, and to plot the king's downfall. Such was the ferocity of her newfound hatred of her husband that at court in England they nicknamed her the 'she-wolf of France'. Crucially for their planned revolt, Mortimer and Isabella had the king's heir, Edward, living with them.

Backed by a mercenary army from Flanders, Isabella and Mortimer invaded in October 1326. Edward fled to Wales, while the queen's forces set themselves up at Gloucester. The following month the queen had her revenge on the younger Despenser. At Hereford, on 24 November 1326, he was cruelly executed. His genitals were sliced off because, contemporary accounts said, 'he was held to be guilty of unnatural practices with the king'. His entrails were cut from him and burned. Finally, he was decapitated and his body quartered. His head was sent to London and the pieces of his body sent to the corners of the kingdom.

Isabella and Mortimer imprisoned Edward II in Kenilworth Castle, and forced him to abdicate his throne. They declared the 14-year-old Prince Edward king. After the coronation, they kept the former King Edward II imprisoned in Berkeley Castle, Gloucestershire, where he met a death matching that of his former lover le Despenser for atrocity.

EDWARD III
1327–1377

 When Edward III became king at the age of only 14, he was little more than a pawn of his power-hungry mother, Queen Isabella, and her lover Roger Mortimer, Earl of March, who had used the boy-king to depose his father Edward II. However, he grew quickly to manhood and shortly before his 18th birthday took power into his own hands. He led a night raid in Nottingham Castle that surprised Isabella and Mortimer as they prepared for bed, sent Mortimer to the Tower and exiled his mother from power and the royal court by despatching her to Castle Rising in Norfolk.

CHAUCER'S KING

Edward proved to be a forceful king, the Christian world's most celebrated warrior of the day. At home he repaired the civil ructions of his father's years and presided over a court in which chivalry, fashion and the finest literature were all celebrated, knights jousted in single combat, courtiers wore extravagant gowns and robes, and the first great English poet, Geoffrey Chaucer, found employment as a civil servant and trusted diplomat.

AT WAR WITH FRANCE

Early in Edward's reign Charles IV of France died without issue and Queen Isabella pressed Edward's claim to the French throne on the basis that Edward was Charles's nephew. The French *parlement* chose Charles's cousin to rule as Philip VI. Initially Edward paid homage to Philip for his French lands, but in 1340 he declared himself King of France. He destroyed the French fleet in July 1340, beginning a prolonged military campaign in France that would later be identified as the first phase of the Hundred Years War (1337–1453).

In 1346 Edward led an invasion of France that climaxed in a famous victory at Crécy on 26 August, when

Above: The Black Prince captured King Jean II of France in the course of the English triumph at Poitiers in 1356.

an army of professional English soldiers and Welsh longbowmen trounced a much larger French force under King Philip VI. Some 10,000 Frenchmen were killed in an encounter that led to just 42 English dead and a few dozen Welsh infantry.

A major figure in Edward's French campaigns was his son Edward, the Prince of Wales, known as the Black Prince because of his black armour. Knighted by his father at the age of 16 in France in 1346, the Black Prince fought bravely that year at Crécy, where he killed the King of Bohemia and took as his own the king's emblem of three feathers and the motto *Ich Dien* ('I serve'). He led the English to another proud victory, in 1356, at the Battle of Poitiers, where an English army of no more than 8,000 defeated a French force of 50,000, killing 13 counts and 66 barons and capturing the French king, Jean II.

From this high point, English fortunes in France declined, for King Edward and his commanders were unable to translate military victories into more lasting power.

EDWARD III, KING OF ENGLAND, 1327–1377

Birth: 13 Nov 1312, Windsor Castle
Father: Edward II of England
Mother: Queen Isabella
Accession: 24 Jan 1327
Coronation: 1 Feb 1327, Westminster Abbey
Queen: Philippa of Hainault (m. 24 Jan 1328; d. 1369)
Succeeded by: His grandson, Richard II
Greatest achievement: Victories over French in Battles of Crécy and Poitiers
26 Aug 1346: Battle of Crécy
17 Oct 1346: Battle of Neville's Cross, Durham
1348: Black Death strikes England
24 June 1348: founds the Most Noble Order of the Garter
19 Sept 1356: Battle of Poitiers
Death: 21 June 1377, Sheen Palace

Above: Regal warrior. This anonymous portrait of the king is at Hampton Court.

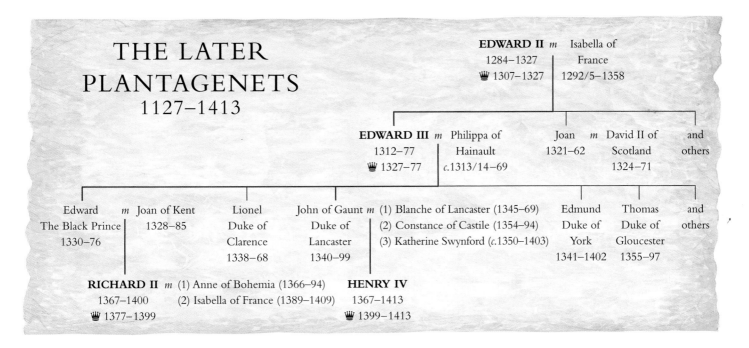

THE LATER PLANTAGENETS
1127–1413

EDWARD II *m* Isabella of
1284–1327 France
♛ 1307–1327 1292/5–1358

EDWARD III *m* Philippa of ⎢ Joan *m* David II of ⎢ and
1312–77 Hainault ⎢ 1321–62 Scotland ⎢ others
♛ 1327–77 *c.*1313/14–69 ⎢ 1324–71

Edward *m* Joan of Kent ⎢ Lionel ⎢ John of Gaunt *m* (1) Blanche of Lancaster (1345–69) ⎢ Edmund ⎢ Thomas ⎢ and
The Black Prince 1328–85 ⎢ Duke of ⎢ Duke of (2) Constance of Castile (1354–94) ⎢ Duke of ⎢ Duke of ⎢ others
1330–76 ⎢ Clarence ⎢ Lancaster (3) Katherine Swynford (*c.*1350–1403) ⎢ York ⎢ Gloucester
⎢ 1338–68 ⎢ 1340–99 ⎢ 1341–1402 ⎢ 1355–97

RICHARD II *m* (1) Anne of Bohemia (1366–94) **HENRY IV**
1367–1400 (2) Isabella of France (1389–1409) 1367–1413
♛ 1377–1399 ♛ 1399–1413

In September 1360 under the Treaty of Brétigny, Jean II was returned to his countrymen – after four years in English captivity – for a ransom of three million gold crowns. Edward renounced his claim to the French throne, while the French recognized English rights in Calais, Poitou and Gascony.

In the following 20-odd years, the French won back many of these lands. Thus, despite heroic victories on French soil, the great warrior king Edward III had fewer French holdings at his death than he had had at his accession.

SCOTTISH KING IN CUSTODY

King Edward also held Scotland's King David II in captivity for almost exactly 11 years after David was captured at the battle of Neville's Cross in 1346.

Earlier in his reign, Edward had provided military backing for the claim of John Balliol's son Edward to the Scottish throne, and in 1334 King David, then just nine years old, was forced to flee to France. In 1341, David had returned to Scotland and then attempted an ill-fated invasion of northern England intended to regain land ceded to Edward III by Edward Balliol.

David was released under the Treaty of Berwick, signed on 6 November 1357, under which the Scots promised to pay a ransom of 100,000 marks for

their king and a ten-year Anglo-Scottish truce was agreed. For a short while in 1356–7, Edward had the strange distinction of holding the kings of both France and Scotland in captivity.

POWER FOR PARLIAMENT

Edward's military campaigns in France and Scotland proved extremely expensive and he needed regular levies of taxation to pay for them. Parliament was in a strong bargaining position and won a number of new powers. These included agreements in 1340 that no new taxes could be imposed without the approval of the Commons in Parliament and, the following year, that the king's ministers would be required to pledge acceptance of Magna Carta and the law in Parliament.

THE BLACK DEATH

The Black Death – a Europe-wide pandemic of bubonic and pneumonic plague – hit England in 1348. It killed the king's favourite daughter, Princess Joan, two archbishops of Canterbury and around one third to one half of the population of the country. As a result of the drastic loss of labour this entailed, the survivors were able to charge more for their labours, leading to severe wage inflation. The 1351 Statute of Labourers once more set wages at pre-1348 levels.

THE ORDER OF THE GARTER

In 1344, Edward III held a round-table tournament at Windsor and took a solemn vow to form an order of Arthurian knights. The Most Noble Order of the Garter, consisting of 26 knights – the king and the Prince of Wales, each with 12 companions – was formed at Windsor on 24 June 1348.

Legend has it that the Order's name and motto derived from a racy incident at a ball in 1347, when a lady – in some accounts the king's mistress, Joan of Kent, Countess of Salisbury – dropped her garter and the king picked it neatly up and tied it around his knee, saying gallantly, *Honi soit qui mal y pense* ('may evil come to the one who has impure thoughts'). St George was the Order's patron saint.

RICHARD II
1377–1399

Richard of Bordeaux, son of Edward, the Black Prince, acceded to the crown of England at the age of 10 in 1377. He had become heir to the throne only the previous year, on the death from dysentery of his warrior father. Richard was crowned amid great pageantry and solemn ceremony on 16 July 1377, watched by his uncle John of Gaunt, Duke of Lancaster, oldest surviving son of the late King Edward III. Until Richard came of age, power was in the hands of a ruling council.

THE PEASANTS' REVOLT

The young king proved that he had inherited his father's courage when he faced down a crowd of angry country labourers at Smithfield on 15 June 1381. The men of Kent and Essex had risen in the 'Peasants' Revolt' to protest against the inequitable poll tax that demanded one shilling from every person, whether rich or poor.

The peasants had arrived in London on 13 June and run riot, demolishing John of Gaunt's palace and the following day storming the Tower of London and executing the Chancellor, Archbishop Simon of Sudbury.

Returning from attending Mass at Westminster on the morning of 15 June, Richard met the rebels in person. When the rebel leader Wat Tyler rode forward to press their demands upon their ruler, he was stabbed to death by the Mayor of London, William Walworth. Tyler's men were about to attack when Richard silenced them with the words, 'Sirs, would you kill your king? I am your king, I am your captain and your leader.' The moment of crisis passed thanks to his bravery and he proceeded to promise sufficient concessions to make the men disperse. Subsequently he would go back on his promises, making the celebrated declaration, 'Villeins ye are, and villeins ye shall remain'.

Richard's early success may have encouraged the traits of arrogance and unwillingness to compromise that led eventually to his downfall. He clashed repeatedly with Parliament and his leading barons, notably over his favourite Robert de Vere, whom he made Duke of Ireland in 1386. Leading barons led by Richard, Duke of Gloucester took up arms in 1387 and issued an appeal to the king to rid himself of de Vere and the Earl of Suffolk, whom they accused of

---

RICHARD II, KING OF ENGLAND 1377–1399

Birth: 6 Jan 1367, Bordeaux

Father: Edward, Prince of Wales ('the Black Prince')

Mother: Countess Joan ('the Fair Maid of Kent')

Accession: 21 June 1377

Coronation: 16 July 1377, Westminster Abbey

Queens: (1) Anne of Bohemia (m. 1382; d. 1394); (2) Isabella of France (m. 1397; d. 1409)

Succeeded by: His cousin, Henry Bolingbroke, Duke of Lancaster

Greatest achievement: Facing down Peasants' Revolt 1381; receiving lords' submission in Ireland 1395

1381: Peasants' Revolt

1387: Uprising of 'Lords Appellant'

1397: Murder and execution of the Lords Appellant Gloucester and Arundel

1398: Exile of Henry Bolingbroke

30 Sept 1399: Deposed in Parliament

14 Feb 1400: Dies in captivity, Pontefract Castle

---

treason. Richard was always unwilling to compromise and called on de Vere to defend the royal cause. At the Battle of Radcot Bridge near Oxford, rebel forces under Gloucester and his nephew Henry Bolingbroke defeated de Vere and forced him to flee. The following year, Gloucester and the leading barons – known as the 'Lords Appellant' because they had issued the 1387 appeal to the king – forced Richard to renew his coronation oaths and at the 'Merciless Parliament' purged the court of Richard's intimates and favourites.

Left: A late 15th-century Flemish chronicle represents the teenage Richard surrounded by his ruling council.

The Lords condemned the exiled de Vere and Suffolk for treason and executed Sir Nichols Bembre, former London mayor, and Sir Robert Tresilian, former chief justice.

Richard waited nine years to have his revenge. In July 1397 the king arrested Gloucester and the Earl of Arundel. He sent Gloucester to Calais, where he was murdered. In September Parliament condemned all the Lords Appellant for plotting against the monarch: Arundel was executed and Warwick exiled. The following year Richard also exiled Henry Bolingbroke for ten years. However, the repercussions of this conflict would bring the king down, for in 1399 Henry Bolingbroke returned to seize the crown and Richard – now deposed – met his end in captivity, possibly at the hands of a murderer in 1400.

DIPLOMATIC SUCCESS

Before the drama of the Lords Appellant had been fully played out, Richard achieved one of the triumphs of his reign. In 1394–5 he led an army to triumph in Ireland and, after spending Christmas in Dublin, received the submission of 80 Irish chiefs, who as a result were confirmed as rulers in their inherited lands. Under the agreement, all land east of a line from Dundalk to Waterford was considered English territory and later called the 'English Pale'. In 1396, moreover, Richard negotiated a 28-year truce with France. At a meeting with Charles VI near Calais, he pledged friendship, promising to support French policy while nevertheless maintaining his claim to the throne.

RICHARD'S MARRIAGES

Richard had two queens. His first was Anne of Bohemia, married in 1382 when both were 15 years old. Although initially a diplomatic match – Anne's father was Holy Roman Emperor Charles IV – this became a close and loving relationship. When Anne died aged just 28 on 7 June 1394, Richard commissioned a truly magnificent

Westminster Abbey tomb with twin effigies of himself and his queen. At her funeral in the Abbey, on 3 August, he was enraged when the Earl of Arundel rudely arrived late, and felled him with his sceptre. In 1397 he made a second diplomatic marriage. As part of the treaty signed with France he took Charles VI's eldest daughter Isabella, aged just seven, as his wife.

Richard was a major artistic patron. He supported poet Geoffrey Chaucer, who had been a diplomat in Edward III's reign and who wrote his poem 'The Parliament of Fowls' in 1382 to celebrate Richard's marriage to Anne of Bohemia. In the 1380s Chaucer was much troubled by debt, and in 1389 he was appointed Clerk of the King's Works, a well-salaried position that brought responsibility for maintaining royal buildings. In 1391 the poet was given work as a forester on the king's lands at North Petherton, in Somerset.

To mark his coming of age Richard commissioned a royal portrait by Andre Beauneveu of Valenciennes to be placed in Westminster Abbey. This image, which represents the king crowned and splendidly robed while holding the royal sceptre, is the first royal portrait painted from life. Richard also rebuilt Westminster Hall from 1393 onwards, adding a porch

Above: In the exquisite Wilton Diptych, Richard kneels beside St Edward the Confessor, St Edmund and a pilgrim, before the Virgin Mary and Christ.

and an oak hammer-beam roof that had the broadest unsupported span in the country. In the 1390s he commissioned a beautiful but anonymous painting, the Wilton Diptych, which he may have used as a portable altarpiece when travelling from palace to palace.

Below: The great poet of Richard's age, Geoffrey Chaucer, was saved from financial troubles by royal patronage.

ACOBVS.QVINTVS.SCOTTORVM.REX &

ANNO.ÆTATIS.SVE.

CHAPTER THREE

RULERS OF SCOTLAND

TO 1603

In 1306, Robert the Bruce, newly established as King of Scots, was in miserable exile in the Western Isles following defeats to English forces at Methven, near Perth, and at Dalry, close to Tyndrum in Perthshire. The old enemy, England, appeared unbeatable, and its vigorous martial ruler King Edward I seemed determined to destroy Scotland as an independent nation and bring its beautiful lands within his own realm.

According to legend, at this low ebb Robert drew comfort from watching a spider as it attempted again and again, undaunted by failure, to spin its web – and finally succeeded. Robert was inspired to fight back, and eight years later he led a Scots army to a famous victory over the English at the Battle of Bannockburn, in 1314. In 1323 he forced Edward I's successor, Edward II of England, to sue for peace. Of course the peace did not last, but Robert is remembered as probably Scotland's greatest king and national hero, 'the Bruce'.

Among the Bruce's lords at Bannockburn was Walter Stewart, scion of a famous family whose name came from their hereditary position as High Steward of Scotland. Walter married the Bruce's daughter Marjorie, and their son, who ruled as Robert II (r.1371–90), founded the great royal house of Stewart (or Stuart, in the French spelling), which was later established by his descendant Mary, Queen of Scots.

In 1603, Mary's son James Charles Stuart united the crowns of Scotland and England when he travelled south to London as King James VI of Scots (r.1567–1603). There he was finally crowned as King James I of England (r.1603–25).

Left: James V took Frenchwoman Mary of Guise as his second queen in 1538. Their daughter was Mary, Queen of Scots.

THE CREATION OF SCOTLAND
TO 1040

The lands now known as Scotland were a military battleground until the 9th century, when King Kenneth mac Alpin forged the first recognizable ancestor of the modern country of the Scots.

ANCIENT FOREBEARS

Four rival groups played an important part in the creation of this country. The first and most venerable were the Picts, present from c.AD300. Little is known about them because their culture was apparently entirely oral; and most of the evidence was destroyed when they were defeated by their rivals in the 9th century. By the 3rd century AD the dozen or so British tribes north of the Forth-Clyde isthmus had merged to form the Caledonians and the Maetae, and it was from these two tribal coalitions the Picts emerged as a recognizable ethnic group.

Celtic Britons made inroads into the south-west of what would become Scotland. The partially Romanized but still independent Britons who lived between the Forth-Clyde isthmus and Hadrian's Wall established a number of kingdoms around the time of the end of Roman rule, most notably Rheged and Gododdin. By c.AD700 they were forced back to the small kingdom of Strathclyde in south-western Scotland.

Above: Scandinavian horseman. This Viking warrior is from a tapestry in Baldishol Church, Norway (1180).

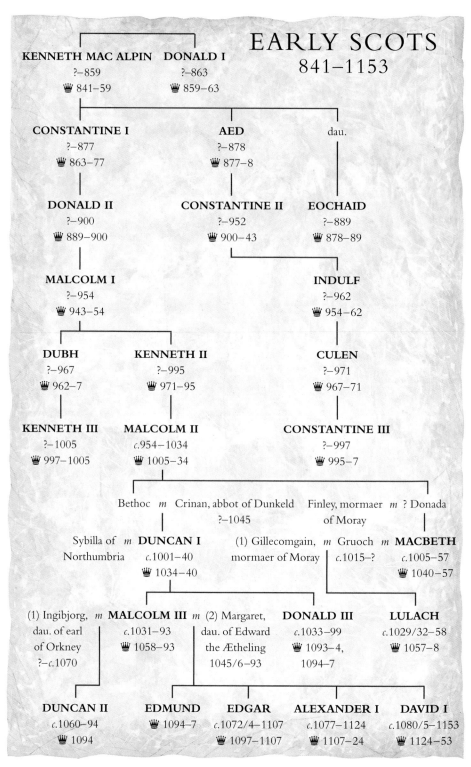

EARLY SCOTS
841–1153

KENNETH MAC ALPIN
?–859
♛ 841–59

DONALD I
?–863
♛ 859–63

CONSTANTINE I
?–877
♛ 863–77

AED
?–878
♛ 877–8

dau.

DONALD II
?–900
♛ 889–900

CONSTANTINE II
?–952
♛ 900–43

EOCHAID
?–889
♛ 878–89

MALCOLM I
?–954
♛ 943–54

INDULF
?–962
♛ 954–62

DUBH
?–967
♛ 962–7

KENNETH II
?–995
♛ 971–95

CULEN
?–971
♛ 967–71

KENNETH III
?–1005
♛ 997–1005

MALCOLM II
c.954–1034
♛ 1005–34

CONSTANTINE III
?–997
♛ 995–7

Bethoc *m* Crinan, abbot of Dunkeld
?–1045

Finley, mormaer *m* ? Donada
of Moray

Sybilla of *m* DUNCAN I
Northumbria   c.1001–40
♛ 1034–40

(1) Gillecomgain, *m* Gruoch *m* MACBETH
mormaer of Moray   c.1015–?   c.1005–57
♛ 1040–57

(1) Ingibjorg, *m* MALCOLM III *m* (2) Margaret,
dau. of earl   c.1031–93   dau. of Edward
of Orkney   ♛ 1058–93   the Ætheling
?–c.1070   1045/6–93

DONALD III
c.1033–99
♛ 1093–4,
1094–7

LULACH
c.1029/32–58
♛ 1057–8

DUNCAN II
c.1060–94
♛ 1094

EDMUND
♛ 1094–7

EDGAR
c.1072/4–1107
♛ 1097–1107

ALEXANDER I
c.1077–1124
♛ 1107–24

DAVID I
c.1080/5–1153
♛ 1124–53

Both Picts and Britons faced incursions into western Scotland from Irish tribes. The Irish established the kingdom of Dal Riada, traditionally under their founding king Fergus Mor (AD498–501), in the area now called Argyll. These people were later called the Scotti (Latin for 'Irish').

The fourth group were the Angles from northern Germany, who arrived as part of the influx of Germanic tribes into Britain in the 5th and 6th centuries AD. They founded the kingdom of Bernicia, which later became part of the northern Anglo-Saxon realm of Northumbria.

FOUNDING FATHER

Scholars often compare the Scottish founding monarch Kenneth mac Alpin to Alfred the Great. Like Alfred, Kenneth forged a united kingdom under persistent threat from Viking invaders, which was consolidated over several reigns. Kenneth's kingdom of Alba was ruled by his brother Donald I (AD859–63), by Kenneth's sons Constantine (AD863–77) and Aed (AD877–8), by their cousin Giric who ruled jointly with Eochaid (AD878–89), by Constantine's son, Donald II (AD889–900), and then by Donald II's nephew and Kenneth's grandson, Constantine II (AD900–43).

In the 9th century the Vikings created kingdoms in Shetland, the western isles and Orkney. The Scots tried to contain the expansionism of Wessex and other 'English' kingdoms in the 10th century. The beginning of English kings' claims to be overlord of Scotland began in AD918 with Edward the Elder of Wessex, who made Constantine II submit to his rule.

Above: Seaborne invaders in the north. This whalebone plaque was found in the boat burial of a Viking chieftain on Sanday, Orkney.

THE STONE OF DESTINY

In AD843 King Kenneth mac Alpin held a sacred investment ceremony on Moot Hill at Scone, ancient royal site of the Picts, using the venerable Irish-Dal Riadan royal stone, the Stone of Destiny. Traditionally the Stone was brought to Scotland from Ireland by King Fergus Mor. According to legend, it originated in the Holy Land and came to Ireland by way of Egypt and Spain. The stone was used for the investment of all Scottish kings until King Edward I of England (1272–1307) removed it from Scone and placed it in Westminster Abbey, where it remained until 1996, when it was finally brought back to Scotland.

Above: The stone was incorporated into Edward I's Coronation Chair.

MACBETH
1040–1057

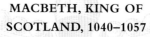

King Duncan I of Scots, grandson of Malcolm II and son of Crinan, the Abbot of Dunkeld, came to the throne in 1034. Six years later he was slain and his crown taken by Macbeth Macfinlay, the ruler of Moray. Shakespeare's tragedy *Macbeth* (probably first performed in 1606) made these royal names among the most resonant in British history, with King Duncan celebrated as the archetype of the wise, noble and divinely ordained ruler and Macbeth as the usurper maddened first by ambition and superstitious belief in prophecy, then by guilt.

FROM FACT TO FOLKLORE

In Shakespeare's play, Macbeth is a brave and well-respected general in King Duncan's army who encounters three witches on a heath and hears their prophecy that he will be made Thane of Cawdor and become king. When Duncan makes him Thane of Cawdor,

Below: Haunted by his misdeeds, Macbeth shies away from the ghost of his fellow general Banquo, whom he murdered.

> **MACBETH, KING OF SCOTLAND, 1040–1057**
> **Birth:** *c.*1005
> **Accession:** 14 Aug 1040
> **Queen:** Gruoch (m. after 1032)
> **Succeeded by:** His stepson, Lulach
> **Death:** 15 Aug 1057 at the Battle of Lumphanan

the prophecy begins to work at him and, encouraged by his wife, Lady Macbeth, he murders Duncan in his bed during the king's visit to his castle.

In fact, as *mormaer* ('ruler' in Gaelic, or high steward) of Moray, the region of northern Scotland around Inverness, Macbeth Macfinlay was a natural rival of Duncan's for power. The Moray *mormaers* were long-term opponents of the kings of Scotland. Moreover, although Macbeth probably had no hereditary claim to Duncan's throne, Macbeth's wife Gruoch and Duncan were third-generation rivals for the throne of Scotland, for Gruoch was granddaughter of King Kenneth III, who had been

Above: Engraver John Boydell (1719-1804) had a romantic vision of Macbeth's encounter with the Three Witches.

killed in battle at Monzievaird in 1005 by Duncan's grandfather, Malcolm II. The historical Duncan does not seem to have been an effective king, for he led several unsuccessful raids into Northumbria, including a failed attack on Durham in 1039. His authority was doubtless weakened by these events.

Duncan's campaign against Macbeth ended in his own death at the Battle of Pitgaveny, near Elgin, on 14 August 1040. Duncan's son Malcolm escaped into exile and stayed first with his mother's relatives at the northern court of Siward, Earl of Northumberland, and then at the court of Edward the Confessor, King of England.

DRAMATIC LICENCE

In Shakespeare's play, Macbeth is unhinged by guilt and fear. He gets drawn further and further into blood-shed as, maddened by new prophecies, he slaughters his fellow general Banquo and the wife and children of Macduff, Thane of Cawdor, against whom he has been warned. Then, in alliance with Duncan's son Malcolm, Macduff invades and kills Macbeth at Dunsinane and Malcolm is proclaimed king.

In fact, Macbeth Macfinlay enjoyed a relatively long and stable rule. He fought several campaigns against the

TANISTRY'S LEGACY OF FAMILY VIOLENCE

For the century prior to the reigns of Duncan and Macbeth, Scots followed a form of succession known as tanistry, under which two branches of Kenneth mac Alpin's family shared the succession. The Scottish throne passed successively from one branch to the other, cousin to cousin or uncle to nephew. The system had the unfortunate effect of fostering violence.

AD943: Constantine II retires to St Andrew's monastery, Fife. He is succeeded by his cousin Malcolm I, who subjugates Moray

AD954: King Malcolm I is killed in Moray uprising and is succeeded by his cousin Indulf

AD962: Indulf is killed by Danes and succeeded by Malcolm's son Dubh

AD967: Dubh is murdered on the orders of his cousin Culen, who succeeds to the crown

AD971: Culen in assassinated in a revenge attack by Dubh's brother; Kenneth II succeeds

AD995: Kenneth II is killed by noblewoman Finvela; his cousin Constantine III succeeds

AD997: Constantine III is killed; Dubh's son Kenneth III succeeds

1005: Kenneth II's son Malcolm kills Kenneth III and takes the throne as Malcolm II

c.1018: Malcolm II acquires Strathclyde and Lothian for Scotland

1034: After a 28-year reign Malcolm II rejects the tanistry tradition and leaves the country to his grandson Duncan.

Above: Cawdor Castle, the supposed site of Macbeth's murder of Duncan, was actually built in the late 14th century.

Norse in Caithness and Sutherland, defeated a rebel force near Dunkeld (modern Tayside) in 1045, killing Malcolm's grandfather Crinan, Abbot of Dunkeld, and in 1046 was victorious over Siward, Earl of Northumbria, who was seeking to elevate Duncan's son Malcolm to the kingship.

On 27 July 1054, however, he was defeated at Dunsinane, near Scone, by Siward and Malcolm and forced to cede Lothian and Strathclyde in southern Scotland to Malcolm. The invasion was supported by the English troops of Edward the Confessor, who had provided hospitality to Malcolm at his court and who envisaged him as a puppet ruler on the Scottish throne. In 1057 Macbeth was killed in battle at Lumphanan, west of Aberdeen, by Malcolm himself. Macbeth's 25-year-old stepson Lulach briefly inherited the crown, but was killed by Malcolm in an ambush in 1058. Macbeth himself was clearly not regarded as a usurper, for he was laid to rest on Iona, which was the burial ground only of lawful monarchs.

Below: Far from being the paragon of noble kingship celebrated by Shakespeare, Duncan was a rather ineffectual ruler.

Below: The historical Macbeth was mormaer of Moray from c.1031 and ruled all of Scotland for 17 years.

THE DEADLY APPLE

Contrary to Shakespeare's account, Duncan was not in truth a victim of treachery in Macbeth's household, but one of his royal predecessors did fall foul of deadly hospitality.

In AD995 King Kenneth II was murdered by or at the instigation of Scots noblewoman Finvela, who blamed him for the death of her only son. According to legend, she invited him to her house and treated him to a great banquet with wine. When her royal guest was drunk, Finvela led him into another chamber, where she had prepared a bizarre contraption: a statue bearing a golden apple connected to a number of hidden crossbows, which were set to fire when the apple was lifted. She invited Kenneth to take the apple as a symbol of their reconciliation and, when he lifted the golden fruit, he was shot.

FROM MALCOLM III TO MALCOLM IV

1058–1165

Malcolm III Canmore ('big head' or 'great leader') regained the throne lost 18 years earlier by his father King Duncan, in 1058, with English backing. The 18-year rule of the lords of Moray – Macbeth Macfinlay (1040–57) and his stepson Lulach (1057–8) – was over. Malcolm had spent the first 14 of those 18 years in exile in England and after returning to Scotland remained involved in the upheavals south of the border.

ENGLISH ALLIANCES

In 1066, when Harold Godwineson became King Harold II of England, Malcolm III Canmore joined the northern invasion raised by Earl Tostig and King Harald Hardrada of Norway. Then, in 1068, following Duke William of Normandy's occupation of the English throne as King William I, Malcolm gave sanctuary in Scotland to another of William's rivals, Edgar the

Left: Edinburgh Castle stands high on a rock above the city. It contains a Norman chapel to St Margaret, wife of Malcolm III.

Above: Might and right. A manuscript of 1588 depicts King Malcolm III of Scots and his pious second wife, Margaret.

Atheling and his mother and sisters. The next year he took one of the sisters, the pious and later sainted Margaret, as his wife. Malcolm raided Northumbria in 1070, and in 1072 William I invaded eastern Scotland with naval backup to punish him. Malcolm made peace rather than engage the formidable Norman army. In a treaty signed at Abernethy, near Perth, on 15 August 1072, Malcolm acknowledged William I's overlordship. He was also forced to send his son Duncan into exile as an English hostage and to expel his brother-in-law Edgar the Atheling from Scotland.

Despite having acknowledged English overlordship, Malcolm again raided Northumbria in 1079, 1090 and 1093. The last attack ended in Malcolm's death in an ambush. Malcolm's son and heir Edward was also killed and a succession crisis was sparked.

Four years of dynastic disputes were ended by the victory in 1097 of Edgar, one of Malcolm's sons with Queen Margaret. During his ten-year reign,

Edgar restored stability. His pious character and patronage of the Church won him the nickname 'Gentle King Edgar' and one contemporary, St Aelred of Rievaulx, declared that he equalled Edward the Confessor in holiness.

Two key events of Edgar's reign were the recognition in 1098 of Norwegian rule in the Hebrides by King Magnus III 'Barefoot' of Norway and the diplomatic marriage in 1100 between England's new king, Henry I, and Edgar's sister Edith (who later took the Norman name Matilda). Edgar himself remained unmarried. At his death, aged 33, on 8 January 1107 he was succeeded by his brother, Alexander.

RISE OF KING DAVID

Alexander I followed his elder brother Edgar's instructions in allowing his younger brother, David, to govern southern Scotland while he himself controlled the north. Alexander maintained good relations with his brother-in-law King Henry I of

ROYAL INFANTICIDE

King David paid a high price for offering hospitality in 1114, when he was governing southern Scotland in his brother Alexander I's reign. David gave houseroom to a Scandinavian priest who had been blinded and had had his feet and hands amputated as a punishment for the brutal sacrifice of a colleague on a church altar in Norway. Sadly the priest proved to be insane: he used the metal hook he wore in place of a hand to cut open and kill David's infant son Malcolm. Wild with a father's grief, David ordered the priest to be tied to horses so that he would be torn apart when they were whipped and sent galloping in different directions.

England, accepted the status of Henry's feudal vassal and entered a diplomatic marriage to Sibylla, Henry's illegitimate daughter. Alexander also fought alongside the English king, leading a Scottish troop during Henry's campaigns in Wales in 1114.

On Alexander's death aged 47, on 23 April 1124, David took power over all of Scotland and ruled as King David I. He had many connections with England. He was brother-in-law to King Henry I through the late Queen Matilda (formerly 'Edith') and was himself married to Maud, daughter of Earl Waltheof of Northumbria. Furthermore, he had lived as an exile at the English court in the 1090s during the succession crisis that followed the death of his father Malcolm III.

In David's reign, Scotland and its monarchy gained a new strength and prestige. He established a central government administration, introduced royal coinage and imported an Anglo-Norman feudal system. Many notable Anglo-Norman lords settled in Scotland, receiving grants of land in return for royal service and intermarrying with the local aristocracy. Celebrated Scottish

families including Bruce, Stewart and Comyn were among the influx of Anglo-Normans that occurred during King David's reign.

David was a great church patron, founding many Cistercian and Augustinian monastic establishments. Several castles and burghs, or fortified settlements, were also raised or rebuilt under his rule, including Edinburgh, Berwick, Roxburgh and Stirling.

Under David, the country grew to its largest extent. After 1130, he succeeded in subjugating the always troublesome earldom of Moray, possession of the descendants of Macbeth Macfinlay (1040–57). In the course of the civil war in England in King Stephen's reign (1135–54), David initially backed Henry I's daughter, the Empress Matilda, but twice made peace with Stephen. He gained Cumberland, Northumberland,

Durham, Westmorland and, for a time, Lancaster for Scotland, a state of affairs recognized by Henry Plantagenet (the future Henry II) in 1149.

SWIFT DECLINE

David's territorial gains in northern England were short-lived, however. He died in Carlisle on 24 May 1153 and, because both his sons were already dead, was succeeded by his 12-year-old grandson Malcolm IV. The youthful king did succeed in subduing Galloway in 1160, and in 1164 put down a rebellion led by Somerled, 'Lord of the Western Isles', at Renfrew, but aside from that, his reign was short and largely uneventful and he died aged only 23.

Below: Growing territory. By the end of King David's reign in 1153, Scotland stretched as far south as the river Tees.

WILLIAM I THE LION
1165–1214

On the unexpected death of the quiet, pious and chaste King Malcolm IV in December 1165, his energetic, red-haired brother William came to the throne. Invested at Scone on Christmas Eve 1165, William would remain on the throne for 49 years, the longest reign of any Scots king in the medieval period. His posthumous nickname, 'the Lion', may derive from his fearlessness and strength in battle, but is more likely to have been a reference to the heraldic device he adopted, of a red lion rampant against a yellow background.

NORTHUMBERLAND CONTROL

The vexed question of Scottish control over Northumberland, gained by William's grandfather David I but lost by Malcolm IV, troubled much of William's reign. Early on, in 1174, William saw an opportunity. Henry II's sons Henry the Young King, Richard and Geoffrey were in open revolt against their father in Normandy, so

Above: In the 14th century, John of Fordun named William leo justitiae *('lion of justice') – a possible source of his nickname 'the Lion'.*

William invaded Northumberland. However, the Scots king was caught unawares in mist when besieging Alnwick Castle. Unable to see clearly, he mistook a group of English cavalry for his own knights. He was surprised and, although he fought valiantly, had

WILLIAM I 'THE LION', KING OF SCOTLAND, 1165–1214
Birth: 1142/3
Father: Henry, Earl of Northumberland
Mother: Ada de Warenne
Accession: 9 Dec 1165
Investiture: 24 Dec, 1165, Scone
Queen: Ermengarde (m. 5 Sept 1186; d. 1233)
Succeeded by: His son Alexander
Greatest achievement: Stability of a 49-year reign
1168: Alliance with France
1174: Captured at Alnwick and imprisoned by Henry II
Dec 1174: Treaty of Falaise: William swears allegiance to Henry II
1178: Founds Arbroath Abbey
1189: Treaty of Falaise cancelled by King Richard I
Death: 4 Dec 1214, Stirling

his horse killed beneath him and was ultimately overpowered. The humiliation of being captured alive was made worse when he was thrown in jail and kept as a prisoner of King Henry II for five months, powerless to prevent the gleeful English troops from plundering southern Scotland.

Below: Stirling Castle. William created a royal hunting ground at Stirling and died in the castle on 4 December 1214.

ARBROATH ABBEY

King William the Lion established the Abbey of Arbroath in 1178 to honour the memory of St Thomas à Becket. Becket had been murdered eight years earlier at Canterbury by knights who were probably acting on behalf of Henry I, and he was canonized only 15 months later in 1172. The Abbey housed monks of the Tironensian order, which originated in Tiron, France, and had Kelso Abbey – founded by King David I – as its main Scottish base. However, the monks of Arbroath were independent of the 'mother house'.

Arbroath Abbey became one of the wealthiest in Scotland. William made the monks many grants of income and also allowed them to establish a fortified settlement, hold a market and construct a harbour. Following his death in 1214, King William was buried at the Abbey. A little over a century later, in 1320, Scotland's resounding statement of independence from England, the Declaration of Arbroath, was signed at the Abbey.

Left: The impressive south transept still stands among the ruins of Arbroath Abbey.

Above: Alnwick Castle, Northumberland, was the site of William the Lion's catastrophic capture by English knights.

Worse still was to follow. The price of William's release was the punitive Treaty of Falaise, signed in December 1174, under which William had to pledge allegiance to Henry as his vassal, to accept that the English Church was supreme over the Scottish Church and to pay for the establishment of English garrisons in Scottish territory. Scotland had become a feudal possession of the English king.

FREEDOM FOR SALE

This state of affairs improved 15 years later when, following the death of Henry II, King Richard I 'the Lionheart' was raising money to fund his departure for the Holy Land on the Third Crusade. Richard I agreed to accept that the Treaty of Falaise had been obtained by force and reversed its terms in return for a cash payment of 10,000 marks.

A little later, the clause of the treaty that had established the supremacy of the English Church was undermined by Pope Celestine III who, in 1192, declared that the Church in Scotland owed allegiance to Rome alone and could not be forced to submit to the English Church.

Following the accession of King John in 1199, William plotted a further invasion to reassert Scotland's claim over Northumberland. According to tradition, the king – who was a pious man – received a divine warning that a major

campaign in northern England would have dire consequences for Scotland. He limited himself to minor raiding, which in itself brought disastrous results. A show of English military strength forced a treaty signed at Norham, Northumberland, on 7 September 1209, in which William again had to recognize the English king as his feudal overlord and allow John to arrange marriages for his daughters.

FRENCH CONNECTION

In 1168 William made an alliance with Louis VII of France that some scholars identify as the beginning of the 'Auld Alliance', the centuries-long diplomatic 'friendship' between French and Scottish monarchs eager to strengthen their position against the English.

At home William built on David's legacy, founding burghs and consolidating a local law system of sheriffs and justices.

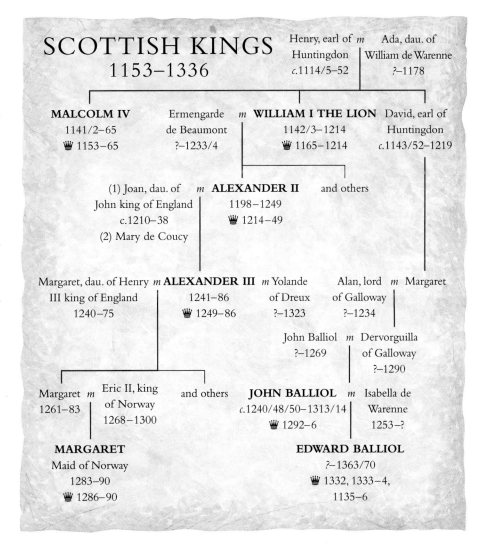

SCOTTISH KINGS
1153–1336

Henry, earl of *m* Ada, dau. of
Huntingdon | William de Warenne
*c.*1114/5–52 | ?–1178

MALCOLM IV
1141/2–65
♛ 1153–65

Ermengarde
de Beaumont
?–1233/4

m **WILLIAM I THE LION**
1142/3–1214
♛ 1165–1214

David, earl of
Huntingdon
*c.*1143/52–1219

(1) Joan, dau. of
John king of England
c.1210–38
(2) Mary de Coucy

m **ALEXANDER II**
1198–1249
♛ 1214–49

and others

Margaret, dau. of Henry
III king of England
1240–75

m **ALEXANDER III**
1241–86
♛ 1249–86

m Yolande
of Dreux
?–1323

Alan, lord *m* Margaret
of Galloway
?–1234

John Balliol *m* Dervorguilla
?–1269 | of Galloway
?–1290

Margaret *m*
1261–83

Eric II, king
of Norway
1268–1300

and others

JOHN BALLIOL
*c.*1240/48/50–1313/14
♛ 1292–6

m Isabella de
Warenne
1253–?

MARGARET
Maid of Norway
1283–90
♛ 1286–90

EDWARD BALLIOL
?–1363/70
♛ 1332, 1333–4,
1135–6

ALEXANDER II
1214–1249

Following the stability of William the Lion's 49-year reign, William's 16-year-old son Alexander came to the throne in 1214. The next year, sensing an opportunity to make progress towards his father's long-held dream of regaining former Scottish territory in Northumberland, Alexander sided with the barons of England when they rose up and imposed the Magna Carta on King John.

THE PEACE OF YORK

Alexander paid homage to Prince Louis, heir to the French crown, who had been offered the English throne. However, John had his revenge, launching a savage attack on Lothian designed, he declared, to 'hunt the red foxcub from his lairs', a reference to the red hair that Alexander had inherited from his father. Following the death of King John in 1216 and the collapse of the baronial rebellion in 1217, Alexander made peace with England's new king, Henry III, paying homage to him for his lands in England at Christmas 1217. Then on 19 June 1221, at York, he married Henry's sister, Joan.

Above: Alexander allied himself to the English barons who in the Magna Carta set limits on his father-in-law King John's authority.

The new harmonious Anglo-Scottish atmosphere resulted in the 1237 Peace of York, under which Alexander renounced his claim to the disputed northern territories, including Northumberland, and the border between the two countries was agreed as running north-east from the Solway to the Tweed – roughly the border that has survived to this day. The peace treaty rewarded Alexander's accommodating approach by giving him rights to a number of English estates.

PEACE AND STABILITY

Alexander II maintained peace for Scotland and his byname became 'the Peaceful'. However, he had to be tough and pragmatic. Like his predecessors, he

Left: Alexander II was warned in a dream not to try to recapture the Hebrides from Norway. He disregarded the advice – and died of a fever while on campaign.

had his work cut out to impose his authority in the west and north-west of his realm. He put down revolts in Galloway in 1234–5 and 1247 and brutally punished rebels in Caithness, in the far north, by ordering that each captured rebel have one hand and one foot cut off. He caught a fever whilst on campaign and died aged 50 in 1249.

ALEXANDER II, KING OF SCOTLAND, 1214–1249

Birth: 24 Aug 1198, Haddington, East Lothian

Father: William I the Lion

Mother: Ermengarde de Beaumont

Accession: 4 Dec 1214

Coronation: 6 Dec 1214, Scone Abbey

Queens: (1) Joan, daughter of King John of England (m. June 1221; d.1238); (2) Mary de Coucy (m. 15 May 1239)

Succeeded by: His son Alexander III

Death: 6 July 1249, on the Isle of Kerrara in the Bay of Oban

ALEXANDER III
1249–1286

Alexander II had reigned for a very respectable 34 years, but his unexpected end was not well timed, for his son and heir, who came to the throne as King Alexander III, was just eight years old.

JUNIOR ROYAL WEDDING

Within three years, at the age of just ten, Alexander III made a major diplomatic match when he was married to King Henry III's 21-year-old daughter Margaret. The ceremony took place on 26 December 1251 in York Abbey and was long remembered, not least for Henry's attempt to take advantage of Alexander's tender years and make him pay homage to the English king for all his Scottish lands. Alexander, canny and well prepared, replied that he was present to be married and 'not to answer about so difficult a matter'.

A DEAL WITH NORWAY

At peace with England, Alexander pressed on with his father's project of regaining control of the Western Isles. In 1263 he offered to buy Kintyre and the Western Isles from King Haakon IV of Norway. Haakon refused and, acting on reports that the Scots had attacked Skye, led a punitive raid along the west coast. His fleet anchored off Largs, near Ayr, but was wrecked in a storm and an invading party was driven back by Scottish troops in a beach battle at Largs on 2 October. On his return from this bungled expedition, Haakon became ill and died in Orkney.

Haakon's successor on the Norwegian throne, King Magnus V, agreed the Treaty of Perth in 1266 under which Scotland regained the Western Isles.

Right: Tradition has it that Colin Fitzgerald, first chief of Clan Mackenzie, saved Alexander III from a stag. Benjamin West imagined the scene in 1786.

In August 1274 King Alexander and Queen Margaret were guests at the coronation of Margaret's brother Edward as King Edward I of England. Alexander was pleased to maintain friendly relations with England, but he would not allow Scotland's independence to be undermined. Visiting Westminster in October 1278, he willingly paid homage for his lands in England to Edward I, but made a proud declaration of Scotland's independence when it was suggested by the Bishop of Norwich that a Scottish king should pay homage to his English counterpart for all his territories. Alexander replied in ringing tones, 'To homage for my kingdom of Scotland no one has right except God alone. Nor do I hold it except of God alone'.

Alexander's Scotland was prosperous, stable and secure, but his sudden death in March 1286 plunged the country into a succession crisis. Riding from Edinburgh to Dunfermline on 19 March 1286, Alexander and his horse fell over a cliff during a storm. With his three children already dead, his only heir was his granddaughter Margaret, the daughter of King Eric II of Norway, and Alexander III's daughter, another Margaret. This infant girl, born only the previous year and known as the 'Maid of Norway', was therefore declared Queen of Scotland.

ALEXANDER III, KING OF SCOTLAND, 1249–1286

Birth: 4 Sept 1241, Roxburgh
Father: Alexander II
Mother: Mary de Coucy
Accession: 8 July 1249
Coronation: 13 July 1249, Scone Abbey
Queens: (1) Margaret, daughter of Henry III of England (m. 26 Dec 1251); (2) Yolande or Joletta, daughter of Robert IV, Count of Dreux (m. 1 Nov 1285; d. 1323)
Succeeded by: Margaret
Death: 19 March 1286

JOHN BALLIOL AND ROBERT I 'THE BRUCE'

1286–1329

Scotland's child-queen, Margaret the 'Maid of Norway', ruled for four years without setting foot in her realm. She died in the Orkney Islands in 1290, aged just seven, as she was travelling to Scotland for the first time. She left a power vacuum in which there were 13 rival claimants for the throne. The strongest of these were John Balliol and Robert Bruce (the grandfather of Robert I Bruce), both descendants of King David I's daughters.

AN EMPTY THRONE

Edward I of England was determined to force the Scots to recognize him as their overlord and sensed a magnificent opportunity in this succession crisis.

At Norham, near Berwick, he acted as mediator between the rivals and chose Balliol, who had the stronger legal claim and who also promised to pay homage to Edward. However, Balliol later defied Edward by choosing to ally

Below: King John Balliol is pictured with the heraldic arms that he had stripped from him by a merciless Edward I of England.

JOHN BALLIOL, KING OF SCOTLAND, 1292–1296

Birth: *c.*1240/48/50, Barnard Castle
Father: John Balliol
Mother: Devorguilla of Galloway
Accession: 17 Nov 1292
Coronation: 30 Nov 1292, Scone Abbey
Queen: Isabella, daughter of John de Warenne, 6th Earl of Surrey (m. before 7 Feb 1281)
10/11 July 1296: Abdicates at Brechin
Death: 1313/14, Normandy

---

with France in the 1295 Treaty of Paris rather than fight alongside Edward in a proposed war against the French. Edward's army invaded Scotland in 1296, sacked Berwick and then crushed Balliol's Scottish army at Dunbar. On 10 July, Balliol was stripped of his knightly arms, crown, sword and sceptre and then despatched to London, where he was cast into the Tower. The event won John the mocking nickname 'Toom Tabard' (vacant coat'), a reference to the removal of his heraldic arms.

For ten years the Scottish throne remained empty. In 1300 Edward I rubbed in his victory by removing the Stone of Destiny from Scotland and using it as part of a newly constructed coronation chair in Westminster Abbey.

Scottish pride was in the hands of rebel leader Sir William Wallace, who defied Edward for eight years, crushing an English army at Stirling in 1297 and later the same year taunting the English king by raiding Northumberland and Cumberland. Wallace was captured in Scotland in 1305, taken to London, condemned as a traitor and brutally executed. His name lived on, however, as an inspiration to those fighting for Scottish independence.

BRUCE TAKES POWER

Meanwhile the Scottish families of Bruce and Comyn (Cumming) were the principal claimants to the vacant Scottish throne. Robert the Bruce (grandson of the Robert Bruce who had lost the crown to Balliol in 1292) seized the initiative. On 10 February 1306 he or his followers murdered his chief rival, John Comyn, in the Franciscan Church at Dumfries. Bruce then had himself crowned King Robert I of Scots, at Scone, on 27 March. He immediately set about eliminating resistance to his rule. However, he received two major and near-immediate setbacks in the form of military defeats by English troops at Methven on 19 June and Dalry, close to Tyndrum, on 11 August. He fled into exile.

VICTORY AT BANNOCKBURN

In 1307 Robert I's prospects improved when his principal adversary, the great warrior-king Edward I, died of dysentery as he was travelling north to invade Scotland once more. Edward I's successor, the hot-headed Edward II, was far less of a threat. In Scotland, Robert I established his own rule over all of the

Above: 'We fight… for freedom alone'. Scotland's independence was declared at Arbroath by Robert I's nobles in 1320.

country save the south-east corner and routed Edward II's army at the battle of Bannockburn, in June 1314.

Edward had led his large army into Scotland to relieve the English garrison in Stirling Castle, which was besieged by Robert I. Greatly outnumbered, the Scots were rallied by King Robert, who told them, 'Fight for your nation's honour'. First with cavalry and then with spearmen, the Scots took the battle to the English. The invading army panicked and broke when King Edward II fled for his life. Thousands of Englishmen were slain.

This remarkable victory over the Plantagenet English army made Robert the Bruce a hero in Scotland, established his claim to the throne beyond doubt, united the Scots and ended the Bruce–Comyn war.

ROBERT I THE BRUCE, KING OF SCOTLAND, 1306–1329

Birth: 11 July 1274, Turnberry Castle, Ayrshire
Father: Robert (VI) de Brus (d. 1304)
Mother: Marjory, Countess of Carrick
Accession: 10 Feb 1306
Investiture: 27 March 1306, Scone
Queen: Elizabeth (m. 1302; d. 1327)
Succeeded by: His son David
Greatest achievement: Safeguarding Scottish independence
10 Feb 1306: Murders rival John Comyn and seizes power
June–August 1306: Military defeats drive him into hiding
24 June 1314: Battle of Bannockburn
1320: Declaration of Arbroath
1328: Treaty of Edinburgh
Death: 7 June 1329, Cardross, Dumbartonshire

DECLARATION OF ARBROATH

In 1320, Robert encouraged his leading nobles to make the resonant statement of Scotland's independence known as the Declaration of Arbroath. The document, drawn up on 6 April 1320, probably by Bernard de Linton, Abbot of Arbroath Abbey and Chancellor of Scotland, was addressed to Pope John XXII at Avignon, who had excommunicated Robert I following the murder of John Comyn and who so far refused to accept Scottish independence. The Declaration stated that the Scots were bound to their King Robert, 'By law and by his strengths, so that we may continue free, and we will continue to stand by him, come what may', but it added that they would drive their king out, 'As an enemy' if he consented to make Scotland subject to England once more. The Declaration also stated that the Scots were fighting not for wealth or glory or worldy status, 'But for freedom – and for freedom only, which no honourable man will give up but with his life'.

Robert's dream was realized in 1328, following the deposition of Edward II and the accession of the youthful Edward III, in the Treaty of Edinburgh and Northampton. England recognized Scotland's independence.

Robert I, great hero of Scottish independence, suffered from illness in his later years and died, probably of leprosy, in 1329. In 1328 the Pope had lifted the writ of excommunication that he had imposed ten years earlier. On his deathbed, Robert arranged to have his heart excized after his death and made Sir James Douglas pledge to take the heart with him on crusade to the Holy Land. The king's body was buried at Dunfermline Abbey and the heart – returned to Scotland after Douglas was killed in Spain en route for the Holy Land – was interred at Melrose Abbey.

Below: Robert I is shown with his first wife, Isabel. Their grandson was Robert II, the founder of the House of Stewart.

DAVID II
1329–1371

Robert I's death in June 1329 plunged newly independent Scotland back into rivalry between Balliol and Bruce as dynastic feuding erupted. John Balliol's son Edward claimed the throne, invaded Scotland, defeated David II's guardian Donald of Mar on Dupplin Moor and was made king in September. In December, barons loyal to Bruce drove Balliol out and reinstated David II.

In March 1333 Balliol invaded again and, with Edward III, defeated the Scots at Halidon Hill on 19 July to regain the throne. David II fled into exile.

Balliol was little more than Edward III's puppet, to whom he paid homage as feudal overlord and ceded large parts of southern Scotland in June 1334. Balliol proved unable to impose his authority on the country. He was deposed once more

DAVID II, KING OF SCOTLAND, 1329–1371
Birth: 5 March 1324, Dunfermline
Father: Robert I the Bruce
Mother: Elizabeth de Burgh
Accession: 7 June 1329
Coronation: 24 Nov 1331, Scone Abbey
Queens: (1) Joan of England (m. 17 July 1328; d. 7 Sept 1362); (2) Margaret Drummond (m. 1363/4; d. 31 Jan 1375)
Succeeded by: His nephew Robert II
Death: 22 Feb 1371, Edinburgh Castle

in 1334, ruled again in 1335–6 but was deposed yet again in 1336, after which he effectively abandoned his pretensions to the Scottish crown.

KING DAVID'S RETURN

After seven years' exile in France, David returned to reclaim the throne in 1341. The Scots army was crushed in 1346 by an English force at the Battle of Neville's Cross, and David took an arrow in the face before being captured and thrown in jail. He remained in English captivity until 1357.

Below: Peace reigns. In the 1357 Treaty of Berwick David II of Scots agreed terms with the powerful Edward III of England.

Family tree

(1) Isabel of Mar *m* **ROBERT I** *m* (2) Elizabeth de Burgh
?–*c.*1302 — 1274–1329 — ?–*c.*1327
♛ 1306–29

Marjorie *m* Walter the Steward — **DAVID II** *m* (1) Joanna, dau. of Edward II, king of England, 1321–62
1297–1316 — 1292–1326/7 — 1324–71 ♛ 1329–71
(2) Margaret Drummond ?–1375

(1) Elizabeth Mure *m* **ROBERT II** *m* (2) Euphemia Ross
?–*c.*1355 — 1316–90 — ?–*c.*1387
♛ 1371–90

ROBERT III *m* Annabella Drummond
1337/40–1406 — *c.*1350–1401
♛ 1390–1406

Joan Beaufort *m* **JAMES I**
*c.*1400–45 — 1394–1437
♛ 1406–37

JAMES II *m* Mary of Gueldres
1430–60 — 1433–63
♛ 1437–60

Margaret of Denmark *m* **JAMES III**
1456/7–86 — 1452–88
♛ 1460–88

JAMES IV *m* Margaret, dau. of Henry VII, king of England
1473–1513 — 1489–1541
♛ 1488–1513

(1) Madeleine of France *m* **JAMES V** *m* (2) Mary of Guise
1520–37 — 1512–42 — 1515–60
♛ 1513–42

(1) Francis II, king of France *m* **MARY** *m* (2) Henry, Lord Darnley, 1546–67
1544–60 — 1542–87 — (3) James, earl of Bothwell, *c.*1535–78
♛ 1542–67

JAMES VI
1566–1625
♛ 1567–1603

BRUCE AND STEWART
1306–1603

ROBERT II AND ROBERT III
1371–1406

 David's ill-starred reign ended in February 1371. He died without offspring and was succeeded by his nephew Robert Stewart.

THE HOUSE OF STEWART
The new king inaugurating a new and subsequently celebrated dynasty was the grandson of the great Robert I through his daughter Marjorie Bruce. Marjorie married the wealthy and powerful Walter Stewart in 1315. His surname derived from the fact that his family had held the hereditary post of Great Steward of Scotland since the reign of David I.

On accession, Robert was a mature man of 55 years, who had been the king's heir apparent for 45 years. During David II's exile and imprisonment Robert had been variously joint-regent and sole regent. In the course of his reign the Scots regained many English-held territories in southern Scotland in 1384 and then launched several raids in northern England, in 1388 winning a

Above: On accession, Robert II was a mature man of 55, who had been David II's heir apparent for 45 years.

long-celebrated victory over an English army led by Henry Percy at the Battle of Otterburn. However, Robert took no part in these heroics and, indeed, left affairs of government to his eldest son John, Earl of Carrick.

THE INEFFECTUAL ROBERT III
Robert II died in April 1390 and was succeeded by Carrick who, on his accession, took the name Robert III because after the years of John Balliol, the name 'John' was considered to be

Below: The circular Rothesay Castle, on the Isle of Bute, was a favoured dwelling of Robert II and his Stewart successors.

unlucky for a king. However, following an accident in 1388, in which he was badly kicked by a horse, Carrick became an invalid no longer fully capable of public life. When he became king, government was largely in the hands of his brother Robert, Earl of Fife and from 1398 Duke of Albany.

Under Albany's venal rule Scotland became a lawless and corrupt place. He tried to refashion the succession, in 1401 arresting and imprisoning his nephew David, Duke of Rothesay, who was heir to the throne. Rothesay died in Albany's castle, according to some accounts from starvation – although an enquiry in 1402 found that he had 'departed this life by divine providence'.

In 1406, to prevent a similar fate befalling the next in succession to the throne, Robert III sent his remaining son, the 11-year-old James Stewart, to safety in France, but James was captured by English pirates, taken to King Henry IV and cast into the Tower of London.

Robert III died later in 1406. He had become a depressive in his later years and famously declared that he could fittingly be buried in a refuse heap beneath the epitaph, 'Here lies the worst among kings and the most wretched of men in the entire country'.

ROBERT III, KING OF SCOTLAND, 1390–1406
Birth: *c.*1337/40
Father: Robert II
Mother: Elizabeth Mure
Accession: 19 April 1390
Coronation: 14 Aug 1390, Scone Abbey
Queen: Annabella Drummond (m. *c.*1366/7; d. *c.*Oct 1401)
Succeeded by: His son James I
Death: 4 April 1406, Dundonald Castle

ROBERT II, KING OF SCOTLAND, 1371–1390
Birth: 2 March 1316, Paisley
Father: Walter the Steward
Mother: Marjorie, daughter of Robert I
Accession: 22 Feb 1371
Coronation: 22 Feb or 26 March 1371, Scone Abbey
Queens: Elizabeth Mure (m. 1336; d. before 1355); (2) Euphemia, Countess of Moray (m. after 2 May 1355; d. 1387)
Succeeded by: His son John, who took the name Robert on his accession to the throne
Death: 19 April 1390, Dundonald Castle

JAMES I
1406–1437

 On the death of King Robert III in 1406, his son James Stewart became James I of Scots at the age of 11. James had been captured that very year while travelling to France to escape potential harm at the hands of his corrupt uncle the Duke of Albany and on accession was in prison in the Tower of London. He became king in exile, but power in Scotland remained in the hands of Albany.

DEATH OF ALBANY

Secure in his position, Albany had little incentive to ransom James; by contrast he did succeed in negotiating the release of his own son, Murdoch Stewart, who was freed by King Henry V of England in 1416. Albany had been the power behind the throne since c.1388–90, but his long 'rule' came to an end on 3 September 1420, when he died aged 80 in Stirling Castle. Murdoch became regent in his stead.

In April 1424, James was freed to return to Scotland, following agreement of a £40,000 ransom to be paid in

Above: Scots king and English rose. While forcibly exiled in England, James I married the beautiful Lady Joan Beaufort.

instalments. Once home, he moved swiftly to impose his authority. On the very day of his return, he is said to have declared, 'If God spares me...I shall see to it throughout the whole of my kingdom that the key keeps the castle and the thorn bush the cow', meaning that property would once again be safe. Within a year he had arrested several rebellious lords and had Murdoch, Duke of Albany executed at Stirling Castle, with two corrupt Stewart kinsmen.

THE POET–KING IN EXILE

James was a man of intelligence, bravery and great ability, and while in England he certainly did not merely rot in prison. He fought in the famous campaigns of King Henry V in France, and he must have won that great monarch's admiration, for in April 1421, Henry invested James as a Knight of the Garter, the prestigious order founded by King Edward III. In addition, James learned about England's developing systems of administration, taxation and government. In 1423 he fell deeply in love with one of Henry's relatives, Lady Joan Beaufort, whom he married in February 1424. Inspired by his love for Joan, James wrote the intense and complex 379-line poem *The Kingis Quair* ('The King's Book'), a work of the highest quality in the tradition of the great Geoffrey Chaucer.

A REFORMING KING

James moved to remodel the Scottish Parliament by increasing the role for lesser nobility (probably in imitation of the House of Commons in Westminster). He greatly improved local justice and instigated reforms of taxation and royal finances. He also had some success in suppressing the independent power of Highland clan leaders. However, on 21 February 1437 he was stabbed to death at Blackfriars Priory in Perth in an attack by several of his leading nobles. They were angered by the king's decision to default on his ransom payments, which had left noble hostages to die in England. James's reputation had also been damaged by his humiliating failure to recapture Roxburgh Castle from the English in a campaign the previous year. The murdered king was succeeded by his 6-year-old son, who ruled as James II.

JAMES I, KING OF SCOTLAND, 1406–1437

Birth: probably late July 1394, Dunfermline Palace
Father: Robert III
Mother: Annabella Drummond
Accession: 4 April 1406 (proclaimed in June 1406)
Coronation: 2 or 21 May 1424
Queen: Joan Beaufort (m. February 1424; d. 1445)
Succeeded by: His son James II
Death: Assassinated in the monastery of Friars Preachers, 21 Feb 1437

Left: James I was a man of many accomplishments – archer, wrestler, athlete, horserider, musician and poet.

JAMES II AND JAMES III

1437–1488

 James II came to the throne at the age of just six. The violent feuding of Scotland's lawless nobility continued throughout his minority, as three leading families – Douglas, Crichton and Livingston – competed for the prince and the crown.

A HOT-HEADED KING

James began to rule as king in 1449, (when he also married Mary of Gueldres) and he dealt severely with his foes, seizing the Livingstone lands. James was a hot-headed young man and in 1452 he murdered William, eighth Earl of Douglas, in a quarrel at Stirling Castle by stabbing him in the neck. He then took on the full might of that powerful family, winning a decisive victory at the Battle of Arkinholm in 1455 and greatly enriching the crown by confiscating the vast Douglas estates.

After 1457, largely secure at home, James turned his attention to the persistent problem of the border with England and led a number of successful military raids against English garrisons. He was killed at Roxburgh Castle, in 1460, when a cannon exploded next to him and blew him to pieces.

JAMES II, KING OF SCOTLAND, 1437–1460

Birth: 16 Oct 1430, Holyrood Palace, Edinburgh
Father: James I
Mother: Joan Beaufort
Accession: 21 Feb 1437
Coronation: 25 March 1437, Holyrood Abbey, Edinburgh
Queen: Mary of Gueldres (m. 3 July 1449; d. 1463)
Succeeded by: His son James III
Death: 3 Aug 1460, killed in cannon explosion at the siege of Roxburgh

---

Above: James II of Scots had a vermilion birthmark on the left-hand side of his face, not shown in this 16th-century portrait.

JAMES III

Scotland was plunged into another minority with the accession of the eight-year-old James III on 3 August 1460. Keen to avoid further feuding, the Scottish parliament awarded custody of the boy-king to his mother, the queen dowager Mary of Gueldres, a strong and devout woman. When she died in 1463, James was under the protection of James Kennedy, Bishop of St Andrews. In 1466 he was seized by Sir Alexander Boyd, Keeper of Edinburgh Castle, who declared himself Guardian of Scotland.

In 1469, James broke free of the Boyds and began to rule in his own right. The same year he wed Margaret of Denmark. A major benefit accrued to Scotland under the marriage treaty, when Denmark agreed to cede the Shetlands and Orkney Islands to Scotland as dowry.

Trouble broke out in the 1470s, when James arrested his brothers Alexander, Duke of Albany, and John, Earl of Mar, accusing them of plotting against him. Mar was killed, while Albany escaped and then returned with

Above: This formal 18th-century portrait of James III of Scots transformed him into a posed, bewigged figure of that later age.

an English army, claiming the throne as Alexander IV. Berwick was captured, Edinburgh sacked and Albany restored to his landholdings, but James continued to reign.

James was killed during another uprising in 1488, by rebels promoting his son the Duke of Rothesay as King James IV. The throne thus passed to yet another youthful Scots king, the 15-year-old James IV.

JAMES III, KING OF SCOTLAND, 1460–1488

Birth: May 1452
Father: James II
Mother: Mary of Gueldres
Accession: 3 Aug 1460
Coronation: 10 Aug 1460, Kelso Abbey
Queen: Margaret of Denmark (m. July 1469; d. 1486)
Succeeded by: His son James IV
Death: 11 June 1488, near Bannockburn

JAMES IV
1488–1513

James IV of Scots became involved in government from his accession, aged 15, in 1488. His efforts to extend the power of the crown into the north and west of the country met with success. In 1493 he humbled the fiercely independent John MacDonald, fourth and last Lord of the Isles, and could boast that his rule extended throughout the Northern and Western Isles.

A RENAISSANCE MAN

James lived up to the ideal of the 'Renaissance prince'. He was a firm and effective ruler who presided over a largely peaceful Scotland and greatly strengthened royal finances: in the course of the reign the king's revenue rose threefold. He was also a renowned patron of the arts and architecture: he built a royal chapel at Stirling Castle and a palace at Falkland and began work on the magnificent Holyrood Palace in Edinburgh. His court became famous throughout Europe as a centre for the arts and the most up-to-date sciences. The king himself was dedicated to medicine and education: he founded King's College, Aberdeen, in 1495, the first British university to have a chair of medicine, and a surgeons' college in Edinburgh. James was also keen on arcane subjects such as alchemy and the possibility of man-powered flight and financed the researches of an Italian

> **JAMES IV, KING OF SCOTLAND, 1488–1513**
> **Birth:** 17 March 1473
> **Father:** James III
> **Mother:** Margaret of Denmark
> **Accession:** 11 June 1488
> **Coronation:** 26 June 1488, Scone Abbey
> **Queen:** Margaret Tudor (m. 8 Aug 1503; d. 1541)
> **Succeeded by:** His son James V
> **Death:** 9 Sept 1513 at the Battle of Flodden

scholar, John Damien, in these areas. He was a keen student of literature and devoured the works of the Scottish poets William Dunbar and Robert Henryson. He also granted a charter in 1507 to Scotland's first printing press.

RELATIONS WITH ENGLAND

In the 1490s James was drawn into the dynastic unrest in England that followed Henry Tudor's seizure of the crown as King Henry VII in 1485.

In 1495 the Scottish court at Stirling welcomed the Pretender to the English throne, Perkin Warbeck, who claimed to be Richard, Duke of York. James became friendly with the imposter, whom he addressed as 'Prince Richard', and even prepared to invade England in support of Warbeck.

In the event, the 'war' was no more than a few raids, and in late 1497 England and Scotland agreed a seven-year truce. Subsequently Warbeck was captured, confessed that his claim was false and was executed on 24 November 1499. The English truce, though, was transformed into a perpetual peace

Left: Stewart wed Tudor when James IV of Scots married Henry VII of England's daughter, Margaret, in August 1503.

Above: James IV, Scotland's first authenticated golfer. Royal accounts in the early 1500s include a record of payment for the king's 'golf clubbis and ballis'.

agreement in a treaty signed in London on 24 January 1502, which also provided for James's marriage to Margaret Tudor, daughter of King Henry VII.

James and Margaret's wedding on 8 August 1503, was celebrated with pageants, tournaments and a poem, 'The Thistle and the Rose', by William Dunbar. Although none can have known this at the time, it paved the way for the union of the crowns of Scotland and England in 1603, when James and Margaret's great-grandson, James Stuart, James VI of Scots, would accede as King James I of England.

The 'perpetual peace' was short-lived. By 1513 Scotland was once more at war with England. When England's King Henry VIII invaded France in 1513, James sent his fleet to Normandy to help Louis XII of France and himself invaded northern England with the Scottish army. The move was a disaster. At the battle of Flodden Field on 9 September 1513, James's army was routed. Around 10,000 Scots were killed, including the king himself.

JAMES V
1513–1542

 Once again Scotland's heir was an infant: James's 17-month-old son, another James, who was crowned King James V at Stirling Castle on 21 September 1513.

FRANCE OR ENGLAND?

In his minority, pro-French and pro-English factions competed for control of king and country. Initially the boy's mother, Queen Margaret, was his guardian but after her marriage to the pro-English Archibald Douglas, 6th Earl of Angus, the pro-French John Stewart, Duke of Albany, was named regent in her place in July 1515.

In 1522, Albany left for France, hoping to raise military backing for an attack on England, and there he remained after a 1524 coup brought the queen's pro-English party back to power. In 1526, Angus captured James and for the following two years kept him captive, but in 1528 James escaped, raised an army of supporters and drove Angus into exile in England.

As king, James set about enforcing his authority. A Catholic at the time of King Henry VIII's break with Rome, he pursued a strongly pro-French policy

THE 'AULD ALLIANCE'

The alliance between Scotland and France that played such an important part in the reigns of Kings James IV and V of Scots was more than two centuries old. Historians usually date the alliance from the 1295 Treaty of Paris, agreed in the reign of John Balliol by leading Scots nobles with King Philip IV of France.

However, some trace the long-standing and intermittently renewed alliance right back to the 1168 treaty between King William I 'the Lion' of Scotland and King Louis VII of France.

The alliance survived the 14th and 15th centuries, but might have been expected to die following the 1502 Treaty of Perpetual Peace with England. Yet James IV renewed the alliance in 1512 in the face of Henry VIII's aggression towards both France and Scotland, and the French alliance was important in the reign of his successor, King James V.

The Auld Alliance had two important side effects. Scots soldiers fought in the French army, particularly after Agincourt (1415). Scottish merchants had a preferential deal on French claret, and so the nobles of Scotland enjoyed finer wine.

Left: James V. In his reign, the Treaty of Rouen renewed the Auld Alliance between Scotland and France.

JAMES V, KING OF SCOTLAND, 1513–1542

Birth: 10 April 1512, Linlithgow Palace

Father: James IV

Mother: Margaret Tudor

Accession: 9 Sept 1513

Coronation: 21 Sept 1513

Queens: (1) Madeleine de Valois (m. 1 Jan 1537; d. 7 July 1537); (2) Mary of Guise (m. 12 June 1538; d. 11 June 1560)

Succeeded by: His daughter Mary

Death: 14 Dec 1542, Falkland Palace

---

and, in 1537, married Madeleine, the 16-year-old daughter of King Francis I of France. She was a frail creature who died only seven months into their marriage, but her vast dowry of 100,000 livres must have been some comfort to James, especially as he was able to negotiate a second prestigious marriage in as many years when he wed the prominent French noblewoman Mary of Guise in 1538.

War erupted with England in 1542 and initial minor successes encouraged King James to invade. At Solway Moss, near Carlisle, on 24 November 1542 the Scots army suffered another catastrophic defeat. Before the year was out the king was dead, aged only 30, devastated by the defeat and the loss the previous year of his two young sons.

Below: According to tradition, James V liked to travel his country in disguise, identified as 'The tenant of Ballengiech'.

MARY, QUEEN OF SCOTS
1542–1567

 When King James V of Scots died in despair at Falkland Palace on 14 December 1542, he had only one heir, his seven-day-old daughter, Mary. She became the first Queen of Scots and the country's youngest-ever monarch. The regency was secured for the tiny queen's French-born mother, Mary of Guise.

A GLORIOUS DESTINY

Mary, Queen of Scots was sent to France at the age of five and there enjoyed a royal education and gilded youth. She grew up a staunch Catholic, speaking French while also learning Latin, Greek, Spanish and Italian, and she became a renowned dancer. As a result of her French upbringing, she changed the spelling of her family name from 'Stewart' to the French form, 'Stuart'.

At the age of 15, in 1558, she married the French heir to the throne, the Dauphin Francis, and with the accession of Queen Elizabeth I of England in November that year, Mary became next

Above: This 19th-century French portrait represents Mary mourning the death of her first husband, Francis II of France.

in line for the English throne too. For Catholics (who did not accept Henry VIII's divorce of Catherine of Aragon and 1533 marriage to Elizabeth's mother, Queen Anne Boleyn), she was the rightful Queen of England. Finally, with the death in July 1559 of Henry II of France from the effects of a hunting wound, her husband Francis became king of France. The young queen's destiny appeared to be glorious.

MISSED OPPORTUNITY

Somehow it all went wrong. Mary loved her young husband, but he died aged only 16 in 1560. She bravely returned home to Scotland and tried without success to find a middle way acceptable to competing Protestant and Catholic camps. She was unable to tame the violent power struggle among competing barons.

Four years after her return, Mary married her handsome but unpopular Tudor cousin Henry Stuart, Lord Darnley, a fellow Catholic who also had a claim to the English throne.

The events of 1566–7 sealed her fate. First her husband Darnley led a group of nobles in butchering Mary's Italian secretary David Rizzio. Next Mary gave birth to a son, James Stuart: while the 'Virgin Queen' Elizabeth I of England remained childless, this boy would be heir to the English throne as well as that of Scotland. Then Darnley was murdered in 1567, perhaps with Mary's involvement, by a group led by the Earl of Bothwell. Mary's marriage to Bothwell in May convinced Scots that she had been involved in Darnley's murder. Rebel nobles triumphed over Mary and Bothwell, and in July 1567 the queen was forced to abdicate in favour of her 13-month-old son.

In 1568 Mary fled to England, seeking sanctuary with her cousin Elizabeth. She was several times the focus of Catholic plots to oust Queen Elizabeth. Mary remained in Elizabeth's custody until her conviction for plotting against Elizabeth's life and was executed on 1 February 1587. After her flight from Scotland she never again set eyes on her only son.

Above: Mary's ill-advised third marriage to James Hepburn, the Earl of Bothwell, forced events that led to her abdication.

MARY, QUEEN OF SCOTS, 1542–1567

Birth: 8 Dec 1542, Linlithgow Palace

Father: James V

Mother: Mary of Guise

Accession: 14 Dec 1542

Coronation: 9 Sept 1543

Husbands: (1) Francis II of France (m. 24 April 1558; d. 5 Dec 1560); (2) Henry Stuart, Lord Darnley (m. 29 July 1565; d. 10 Feb 1567); (3) James Hepburn, fourth Earl of Bothwell (m 15 May 1567; d. 14 April 1578)

Abdicates: 24 July 1567

Succeeded by: Her son James I and VI

Death: Executed 8 Feb 1587

JAMES VI OF SCOTS
1567–1603

 James VI of Scots was crowned aged one year on 29 July 1567 in a church by the gates of Stirling Castle, where he was being kept. In Scotland a succession of four regents – the earls of Moray, Lennox, Mar and Morton – took power. Meanwhile, James received a thorough classical and Protestant religious education, studying Latin, Greek and French under the guidance of his tutor, the learned scholar George Buchanan.

At the age of 16, in August 1582, James was kidnapped by Protestant nobles led by the first Earl of Gowrie, to prevent him falling further under the spell of his Catholic friend Esmé Stuart, the French-born Duke of Lennox and specifically to avert a rumoured plot in which Lennox would force James to convert to Catholicism and then mount an invasion of England. However, James escaped after ten months confinement, and thereafter ruled in his own name.

THE ANGLO-SCOTTISH PACT

As King of Scots, James VI set about cultivating a good relationship with England and in particular with Queen Elizabeth I, with a view to bolstering

---

JAMES VI, KING OF SCOTLAND, 1567–1603; KING OF ENGLAND AND SCOTLAND 1603–1625

Birth: 19 June 1566, Edinburgh Castle

Father: Henry Stuart, Lord Darnley

Mother: Mary, Queen of Scots

Accession: 24 July 1567

Coronation: 29 July 1567

Queen: Anne of Denmark (m. 23 Nov 1589; d. 2 March 1619)

Succeeded by: His son Charles I

Death: 27 March 1625, Theobalds Park, Herts

THE DIVINE RIGHT OF KINGS

James VI was a highly educated intellectual as well as a largely effective, practical king. In September 1598 he published a theory of kingship in his *The Trew Law of Free Monarchies: Or the Reciprock and Mutuall Dutie Betwixt a Free King and his Naturall Subjects*. He argued that kings rule by divine right and are responsible to the Almighty for their actions: 'Kings are called gods by the prophetical King David (the Biblical Psalmist David) because they sit upon God's throne on Earth and have the account of their administration to give unto him'. Their duty is to 'minister justice', 'advance the good and punish the evil', 'establish good lawes' and 'procure the peace of the people'. It follows that subjects have no right to rebel. James urged his people to 'arme your selves with patience and humilitie', adding that since God 'hath the only power to make [a king]' he also 'hath the onely power to unmake him' and subjects' duty was 'onely to obey'. This assertion was to cause a lot of trouble for James' successors.

---

his chances of succession to the English throne after her death. In May 1585 the two monarchs agreed a defensive peace treaty under which James received £4,000 annually. Even Elizabeth's execution of James's mother, Mary, Queen of Scots two years later in 1587 did not seriously disturb the new Anglo-Scottish pact. Although James made a formal complaint about the execution, he knew that his mother's death made him next in line for the English throne.

In Scotland James maintained a strong rule, successfully managing rival Protestant and Catholic sections of the nobility, and establishing his authority as head of the Presbyterian Church.

When, as he had long planned, James acceded to the throne of England on the death of Queen Elizabeth I in 1603, he had been on the throne for 36 years; quite an achievement in the wildly unstable environment of late 16th-century Scotland; and as he told the English Parliament, he was already, 'An old and experienced king'.

Right: This portrait of James VI was sent to the Danish court during negotiations for his marriage to Anne of Denmark.

Above: The two sides of the Jacobus 6 Dei Gratia Rex Scotorum, a gold 'hat piece', worth £4, minted in Edinburgh in 1591.

CHAPTER FOUR

LANCASTER AND YORK

1399–1485

A leading baron and a warrior, Henry Bolingbroke elevated martial vigour above the right of hereditary succession to the throne in the summer and autumn of 1399. Having returned from the exile into which King Richard II had cast him, Bolingbroke led a rebel army to London and forced the king to abdicate in Parliament before claiming the throne himself. When Bolingbroke was crowned King Henry IV in Westminster Abbey on 13 October 1399, he founded the House of Lancaster, a cadet or junior line of the House of Plantagenet. Henry IV's claim to the throne was as the son of John of Gaunt, fourth son of King Edward III. John of Gaunt had married Blanche, the heiress to the duchy of Lancaster, so his son Bolingbroke was Duke of Lancaster.

The king he deposed, Richard II, was his cousin.

The usurper king's dynasty lasted for the reigns of three monarchs – Henry IV himself, his son Henry V, the battle-winning hero of Agincourt, and his ineffective grandson Henry VI who ascended the English throne at the age of just nine months.

The decline of Henry VI into madness led to the elevation of the ambitious Richard, Duke of York, to the role of Protector and Defender of the Kingdom in March 1454. Richard himself had a viable claim to the throne as the great-grandson of King Edward III through the male line via Edmund of Langley, 1st Duke of York (1341–1402). The bitter Wars of the Roses in the second half of the 15th century were fought between the supporters of the rival 'Yorkist' and 'Lancastrian' claims to the throne.

Left: Henry IV was a usurper, but he made sure that his magnificent coronation stressed his majesty and divine appointment to the throne.

HENRY IV
1399–1413

Henry IV claimed the throne of England on the basis of his descent from King Edward III, but the claim was distant. Henry was the son of King Edward's fourth son, John of Gaunt, and Blanche, daughter of the Duke of Lancaster. His claim thus came through the male line. However, if a claim through the female line were allowed, as it had been before, then Edmund Mortimer, Earl of March, had a stronger claim, as the great-grandson of King Edward III's second son, Lionel Duke of Clarence through Lionel's daughter Philippa, Countess of Ulster. Also in his favour was the fact that Richard had recognized him as his heir presumptive. In fact, Henry's most compelling claim to the throne lay in his person; in 1399 he was an accomplished soldier and a man of drive, wealth and education while Edmund Mortimer was a boy of less than 10.

STRUGGLE FOR SUCCESSION

Henry could also claim to have been wronged by Richard II. Henry was one of the Lords Appellant, who had challenged Richard's rule in 1387 and forced the king to restate his coronation

Below: The English gold noble coin was inscribed with a king standing on a ship. First issued by Edward III in 1344, this one was minted for Henry IV in 1412.

HENRY IV, KING OF ENGLAND, 1399–1413

Birth: 3 April 1367, Bolingbroke Castle
Father: John of Gaunt, Duke of Lancaster
Mother: Blanche of Lancaster
Accession: 30 Sept 1399
Coronation: 13 Oct 1399, Westminster Abbey
Queens: (1) Mary de Bohun (m. 5 Feb 1381; d. 1394); (2) Joan of Navarre (m. 7 Feb 1403; d. 1437)

Succeeded by: His son Henry V
Greatest achievement: Founding the House of Lancaster
30 Sept 1399: Richard II deposed
21 July 1403: Defeats rebels at Battle of Shrewsbury
1406: Develops mystery illness – leprosy?
1409: Captures Harlech Castle to end long-running Welsh revolt
Death: 20 March 1413, Westminster

---

oath the following year. He suffered when the king revenged himself in the late 1390s. Richard exiled Henry for ten years in 1398, and in the following year seized Henry's inheritance on the death of John of Gaunt.

On 4 July 1399, while King Richard was campaigning in Ireland, Henry landed from France near Spurn Head with a force of 300 men. Initially he claimed he wanted only to regain his rightful inheritance but as he marched southwards and his army swelled with supporters his demands rose. By then Richard was in hiding in Wales, following his return from Ireland; when the king finally arrived in London, Henry cast him into the Tower.

On 30 September 1399, Richard II was deposed in parliament and the following month Henry was crowned King Henry IV in Westminster Abbey. Richard was imprisoned in Pontefract Castle. The deposed king – no longer Richard II, but merely Richard of Bordeaux – died in jail early the following year, apparently brutally put to death on the orders of Henry IV.

REBEL CHALLENGES

Henry defeated two major uprisings in his reign. His principal opponents were the Welsh prince Owain Glyndwr and the Percy family of Northumberland.

Early in the reign, Glyndwr, Lord of Glyndyfrydwy, declared himself Prince of Wales and gathered support for an uprising against English rule. Despite a largely successful attack on Wales in autumn 1403 and a series of raids led by the English Prince of Wales, the 16-year-old heir to the throne, Prince Henry, the rebellion remained a thorn in Henry's side until 1409.

The Percys were Henry's former allies. They rose in revolt because they believed that the king had failed to reward them sufficiently for their past

Below: Princely patriarch. John of Gaunt, son of Edward III, founded the House of Lancaster through his son, Henry IV.

Above: Froissart's Chronicles *depicts Henry riding into London, the English crown within his grasp.*

in 1406 Glyndwr, Sir Edmund Mortimer, the younger Edmund's uncle, and the Percys agreed to split England between them in the event that they defeated Henry. The rebels, however, suffered a decisive defeat at the Battle of Bramham Moor in February 1408, after which Hotspur's father, the Earl of Northumberland, was executed. In 1409 the king's capture of Harlech Castle effectively ended the Welsh revolt, reducing the proud prince Glyndwr to a landless rebel who had no choice but to hide in caves. His place and date of death are unknown.

TROUBLED IN OLD AGE

Victory did not bring Henry peace of mind or body. Beginning in 1406, he suffered an agonizing illness that may have been leprosy and was identified by some as the judgement of God, perhaps for the murder of Archbishop Scrope of York. Henry was also increasingly at odds with his son, Prince Henry, partly because of rumours in 1411–12 that the prince was plotting to take the throne from his father.

In these later years, the formerly ruthless and ambitious Henry Bolingbroke became careworn and tormented by guilt. As early as 1409, in his will, he declared, 'I Henry, sinful wretch,

Above: The young man who seized the crown spoke French, Latin and English. He holds the red rose of Lancaster.

support, so they rallied around the claim to the throne of Edmund Mortimer, Earl of March. However, in July 1403 the king defeated a rebel army led by Henry Percy ('Hotspur'), warrior son of the Earl of Northumberland, in the Battle of Shrewsbury.

The rebellion continued. In 1405, conspirators Thomas Mowbray and Richard Scrope, Archbishop of York, were captured and put to death. Then

ask my lords and true people forgiveness if I have misentreated them in any wise'. He died on 20 March 1413 after fainting before the Westminster Abbey shrine to his saintly predecessor on the English throne, Edward the Confessor. He was given the last rites and died in the 'Jerusalem Chamber' in the abbot's house at Westminster. His death thus fulfilled a prophecy that the king would die 'in Jerusalem'.

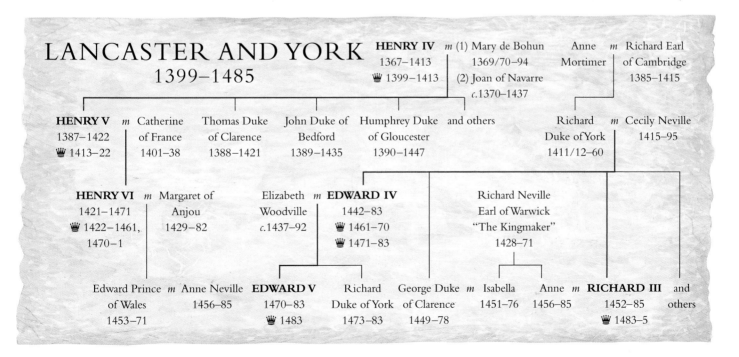

LANCASTER AND YORK
1399–1485

HENRY IV *m* (1) Mary de Bohun 1367–1413 / 1369/70–94 ♛ 1399–1413 / (2) Joan of Navarre *c.*1370–1437		Anne Mortimer *m* Richard Earl of Cambridge 1385–1415	

| **HENRY V** *m* Catherine 1387–1422 / of France ♛ 1413–22 / 1401–38 | Thomas Duke of Clarence 1388–1421 | John Duke of Bedford 1389–1435 | Humphrey Duke of Gloucester 1390–1447 | and others | Richard *m* Cecily Neville Duke of York / 1415–95 1411/12–60 |

| **HENRY VI** *m* Margaret of 1421–1471 / Anjou ♛ 1422–1461, / 1429–82 1470–1 | Elizabeth *m* **EDWARD IV** Woodville / 1442–83 *c.*1437–92 / ♛ 1461–70 / ♛ 1471–83 | Richard Neville Earl of Warwick "The Kingmaker" 1428–71 |

| Edward Prince *m* Anne Neville of Wales / 1456–85 1453–71 | **EDWARD V** 1470–83 ♛ 1483 | Richard Duke of York 1473–83 | George Duke *m* Isabella of Clarence / 1451–76 1449–78 | Anne *m* **RICHARD III** 1456–85 / 1452–85 ♛ 1483–5 | and others |

HENRY V
1413–1422

Henry V led a bedraggled 6,000-strong army in one of the greatest and most celebrated military exploits in English history – the defeat of a French force more than three times larger, at the Battle of Agincourt, on 25 October 1415. His victories during a whirlwind, four-month campaign in France that autumn won him an enduring place in English history and also set the scene for the remarkable treaty signed at Troyes on 21 May 1420, under which Henry was made French regent and recognized as heir to the throne of France.

Before he was king, Henry had made declaration of his martial vigour. He took the fight to Welsh rebel Owain Glyndwr in 1400, when in his early teens, and in 1409 aged 21, he won decisive victories at Aberystwyth and Harlech. When Henry IV lay dying, young Henry took the crown from his father's head, but his father, rallying, asked him what right he had to the crown since it had been won in blood and not received through a divinely blessed hereditary line. The future Henry V told the ailing king, 'As you have kept the crown by the sword, so will I keep it while my life lasts'.

A REFORMED CHARACTER

Henry was crowned King Henry V in Westminster Abbey on Passion Sunday, 9 April 1413. A blizzard enveloped the

Above: Henry married Catherine, daughter of Charles VI of France, on 2 June 1420. James I of Scots was a wedding guest.

Right: Henry V's campaigns in France yielded memorable victories that led to the triumph of the Treaty of Troyes.

HENRY V, KING OF ENGLAND, 1413–1422

Birth: 16 Sept 1387

Father: King Henry IV of England

Mother: Mary de Bohun

Accession: 20 March 1413

Coronation: 9 April 1413, Westminster Abbey

Queen: Catherine of France (m. 2 June 1420; d. 1438)

Succeeded by: His son Henry of Windsor

Greatest achievement: Battle of Agincourt 1415, Treaty of Troyes 1420

25 Oct 1415: Wins Battle of Agincourt

c.1416: Death of Owain Glyndwr

21 May 1420: Becomes regent of France and heir to the French king Charles VI

Death: 31 Aug 1422, Castle of Bois-de-Vincennes, France

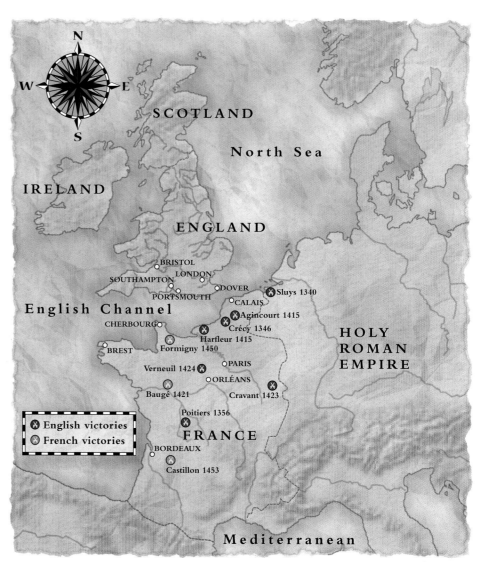

English victories
French victories

THE KING'S FRIEND EXECUTED FOR HERESY

Sir John Oldcastle became a friend of the Prince of Wales during the campaigns against Owain Glyndwr in Wales in Henry IV's reign. However, this did not save him from a heretic's death in 1417.

Oldcastle was executed under Henry IV's 1401 statute 'On the burning of heretics'. He was condemned as a 'Lollard', a member of a group of religious reformers inspired by John Wyclif (d. 1384). Wyclif rejected the doctrine of transubstantiation and argued that the Church and its priests should reject wealth and power and adopt material poverty. Lollards got their name, which derived from a Dutch word meaning 'mumbler', because many of them prayed aloud. Some were a direct political threat to the monarchy, since they proclaimed the rightful king, Richard II, was still alive and living in Scotland. Oldcastle was condemned as a heretic in 1413, but escaped from the Tower of London and remained at large until his capture and execution in 1417.

William Shakespeare transformed Oldcastle into the character of Sir John Falstaff in the *Henry IV* plays. Falstaff is referred to as 'my old lad of the castle', but has none of Oldcastle's controversial religious beliefs.

Abbey, and during the new king's coronation feast onlookers noted that he looked serious and severe and did not indulge in the splendid feast laid out on the banqueting tables before him. As Prince of Wales, Henry had been celebrated for the raucous company he kept and for their wild escapades. Famously, he was involved in a midnight brawl in an Eastcheap tavern, and he also laid ambushes for members of the royal household. Upon his coronation he decisively put his wild years behind him however, declaring that none of his former companions were permitted to come within 10 miles (16km) of him.

WAR IN FRANCE

Henry declared his intention of fighting for the throne of France in early July 1415. He laid claim to the French crown as great-grandson of Edward III, whose mother was the daughter of French king Philip IV. He saw an opportunity to be grasped in France, where the king, Charles VI, was intermittently subject to bouts of madness. Henry set sail in August, besieged and captured Harfleur, then marched for Calais. He defeated the French at Agincourt, then returned to great acclaim from his countrymen, who shouted, 'Welcome, Henry V, King of England and France' as he rode through the city of London. In a second campaign in 1417–19, Henry captured Caen and Rouen, capital of Normandy. Under the Treaty of Troyes he then married Catherine, daughter of the French King Charles VI, and was thereby recognized as heir to the French throne and installed as regent for the French king's periods of madness. But Henry had to fight on to counter the threat presented by King Charles's son, the Dauphin Charles, who was disinherited by this treaty.

Henry's queen, Catherine of France, gave birth to a son, Henry, on 6 December 1421 at Windsor. As Henry

Above: Warrior king. Henry sported a soldier's haircut; such was his athleticism, he was said to be able to outrun a deer.

lay dying the following year of dysentery contracted during the siege of Meaux, near Paris, he appointed his brothers as regents of his domains. Humphrey, Duke of Gloucester, was appointed regent of England, and John, Duke of Bedford, became regent of France. Henry died at the age of just 35.

Below: On 25 October 1415, at the Battle of Agincourt, Henry V's army of 6,000 defeated a French force of 20,000. The victory entered English folklore.

HENRY VI
1422–1461, 1470–1471

 The unexpected death of Henry V thrust greatness on his infant son. Coming to the throne at the age of just nine months, Henry VI set a record (which stands to this day) as the youngest ever king of England.

At first government was in the hands of the young king's uncle, Duke Humphrey of Gloucester, who had been appointed regent by Henry V. Gloucester was soon in open conflict with Henry Beaufort, Bishop of Winchester and Chancellor of England, for control of the boy-king and of the country. Henry was unable to provide the strong rule needed to safeguard the achievements of his illustrious warrior father. Even when he came to adulthood, his character prevented him from becoming master of events and establishing authority over the squabbling barons who surrounded him. For the king was simple, pious, easily swayed and, like his maternal grandfather, King Charles VI of France, subject to bouts of madness. Henry VI's reign was a long, slow decline from the position of considerable strength he inherited.

Below: Joan of Arc said she was guided by Sts Michael, Catherine and Margaret in her campaign against the English in France.

A decline in which England lost its holdings in France and slid into the violent dynastic conflicts that came to be known as the 'Wars of the Roses'.

DISASTERS IN FRANCE
In the spring and early summer of 1429, a French peasant girl known as Joan of Arc led the French army in a string of

Above: Boy among men. Even as an adult, Henry VI was never equal to the task of ruling 15th-century England.

remarkable triumphs against the English. Then in July, the Dauphin, Charles, son of the French King Charles VI, was crowned King Charles VII of France. This coronation was in direct

HENRY VI, KING OF ENGLAND, 1422–1461, 1470–1471

Birth: 6 Dec 1421, Windsor Castle
Father: King Henry V of England
Mother: Queen Catherine of Valois
Accession: 31 Aug 1422
Coronation: 6 Nov 1429, Westminster Abbey; 16 Dec 1431 (as King of France), Notre Dame de Paris
Queen: Margaret of Anjou (m. 22 April 1445; d. 1482)
Succeeded by: Edward IV
Greatest achievement: Founding

King's College, Cambridge, and Eton College
1450: Jack Cade's rebellion
17 July 1453: English defeated at Battle of Castillon
22 May 1455: Battle of St Albans
4 March 1461: Deposed by Edward IV
3 Oct 1470: Restored to throne
11 April 1471: Deposed once more
Death: 21 May 1471, probably murdered, Tower of London

Above: In 1450, Jack Cade's rebels called for the recall of Richard, Duke of York and the dismissal of several ministers.

contravention of the 1420 Treaty of Troyes, which guaranteed the French crown to King Henry V's son and his descendants. In order to counter this, the 10-year-old Henry VI was taken to Paris and crowned as Henri II, King of France, in December 1431. By this time Joan of Arc had been captured, tried for heresy and burnt at the stake in Rouen. Despite her personal fate, Joan had done much to restore French pride.

In 1435 English hopes in France suffered a double blow. The Duke of Burgundy, previously a key ally of England, made peace with the Dauphin. Then Henry VI's uncle, the Duke of Bedford and regent of France, died in Rouen. The Dauphin's army captured Paris from the English in 1436.

In August 1443, Henry – by now 21 years old and ruling in his own right – despatched an English army to France under the command of John Beaufort, Duke of Somerset. The following year, the two countries negotiated a five-year peace and Henry VI married Margaret, daughter of the Duke of Anjou. However, England's French possessions continued to dwindle. Within six

months of the wedding, at the urging of his forceful his new queen, Henry agreed to hand over the duchy of Maine to Margaret's father, René of Anjou. War resumed in 1448-9 and the English lost Normandy in 1450 and Bordeaux and Gascony in 1451. The English sent a force to recover Gascony but the French won a decisive victory at Castillon in July 1453, finally bringing to a close the conflict of the Hundred Years War and leaving Calais England's only remaining French possession.

A PATRON OF EDUCATION

Henry's authority dwindled at home. In 1450 Jack Cade, a former soldier going under the name of 'John Mortimer', led a rebel force of labourers towards the royal court. As Henry fled to the north, the rebels ran riot in London. They were only dispersed when the intrepid Queen Margaret, who had remained in London, offered them pardons.

Henry's mild and pious character may have ill fitted him to be an effective king in late medieval England, but his devoutness inspired him to be a great educational patron, the founder of two

Below: 101 years' work. The magnificent chapel in King's College, Cambridge, was begun in 1446 and completed in 1547.

A SECRET WEDDING

King Henry V's widow, Catherine of Valois, kept her marriage to a Welsh squire secret for six years before it was discovered in 1436. After mourning Henry's untimely death, Catherine settled at Baynard's Castle, at Blackfriars in London. Here, despite a 1428 law declaring that the dowager queen could marry only with the king's consent, in 1430 she secretly wed a Welsh squire named Owain ap Maredudd ap Tudor, better known as Owen Tudor. The couple had a daughter and three sons before their union was discovered. To escape public shame Queen Catherine retired to the nunnery at Bermondsey; meanwhile Owain was cast into Newgate Prison, but escaped in 1438 and returned home to Wales.

major English institutions. In 1440, he established the King's College of Our Lady of Eton, later known as Eton College, and in 1441 he laid the foundation stone for King's College, Cambridge. Generous royal funding provided free education for the 25 poor scholars and 25 paupers at Eton; they were expected to proceed to King's College to complete their education.

THE WARS OF THE ROSES
ENGLAND AT WAR, 1455–1485

 The weak rule of King Henry VI made England vulnerable to power struggles and civil conflict. The king was unable to stamp his authority on the feuding barons around him, who included the ambitious Duke of York, his backer Richard Neville, the Earl of Warwick (later known as 'Warwick the kingmaker') and royal favourites the dukes of Suffolk and Somerset. The barons came into increasingly open competition. Following Suffolk's death in 1450, the struggle was between York and Somerset. The king's susceptibility to periods of madness tipped the balance and a tense standoff eventually erupted into open conflict.

Below: After a defeat for the Yorkist cause at Ludford Bridge in October 1459, the future Edward IV fled to Calais.

Above: The Wars of the Roses are named from the badges of the opposing sides: a red rose for Lancaster and a white rose for York.

THE SLIDE TO CIVIL WAR

King Henry's first attack of insanity in 1453 followed hard on the loss of England's possessions in France. Henry became incapable of making decisions or holding reasoned debate. Richard, Duke of York, was named Protector and Defender of the Kingdom in March 1454 and at once imprisoned Somerset. However, in 1455, after regaining his clarity and sense of purpose, Henry resumed royal rule and released Somerset from the Tower of London.

York rebelled against the king in an attempt to recover his lost authority. On 22 May 1455, York defeated the 'Lancastrian' forces of the king and Somerset at St Albans. As fighting raged in the town, Somerset was trapped in the Castle Inn and put to the sword by Yorkist soldiers. King Henry was shot in the neck with an arrow but managed to escape to safety in the home of a local tanner. York found him there and swore loyalty to his monarch before escorting him from the battlefield to St Albans Abbey and then to London.

The battle was no more than a skirmish, but it marked the beginning of the 33 years of dynastic and political instability and occasional civil war that would be remembered as the Wars of the Roses. In these wars, Lancastrians loyal to King Henry VI and the royal House of Lancaster fought with Yorkist supporters of Richard, Duke of York. The Duke of York had a valid claim to the throne, for he was the nephew of Edmund Mortimer, Earl of March, who had been excluded from the succession when Henry IV seized the throne.

At first the Yorkists had the upper hand. The Duke of York became Constable of England in May, following the St Albans battle, and in November was made Protector for the second time. However, the following year he was deprived of the Protectorship once more as Queen Margaret and her Lancastrian allies manoeuvred against him. In 1458 Henry enforced a reconciliation between the warring parties.

Above: King Henry VI is captured by the forces of Richard, Earl of Warwick, after the Battle of Northampton, in 1460.

Right: Major battle sites of the Wars of the Roses. The conflict was fought out over 30 years and virtually the whole of England.

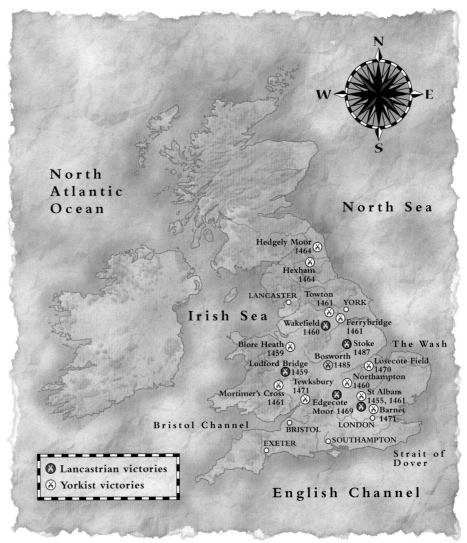

On 25 March – remembered as 'Loveday' – Yorkists and Lancastrians were made to walk in procession, hand in hand, to St Paul's Cathedral in London, and the Yorkists were forced to agree to compensate the descendants of those harmed at St Albans. However, the king was not strong enough to impose peace for long and the following year battle recommenced. After an initial victory at Blore Heath on 23 September, the Yorkists suffered a devastating defeat in the Battle of Ludford Bridge on 12 October. The Duke of York fled to Ireland and in November was condemned as a traitor by Parliament.

A YEAR OF MIXED FORTUNES

In 1460 the Yorkists experienced both triumph and despair. On 10 July, at Northampton, a Yorkist army led by Richard Neville, Earl of Warwick, and the Duke of York's son, Edward, Earl of March, trounced the Lancastrian-royalist forces and captured Henry VI. This appeared to be a decisive victory: York returned from Ireland and in the Act of Accord of 24 October, was named as the heir to Henry VI. However, the ever-resourceful Queen

Margaret orchestrated a Lancastrian response and the pendulum swung in her favour before the year was out.

The queen's army, led by Somerset, defeated the Yorkists at Wakefield in December and killed Richard, Duke of York. The Lancastrians, on Margaret's orders, cut off his head and displayed it in a paper crown on the gates of York. On 17 February 1461, back at St Albans, her army defeated Warwick and rescued Henry VI from captivity. Just two weeks later, the Yorkists gained the upper hand. Warwick and Edward of York entered London and on 4 March Edward declared himself King Edward IV.

YEARS OF CONFLICT

Edward IV ruled with a firm hand for 22 years, establishing the new dynasty of the House of York. However, the country endured two further bouts of bloody dynastic conflict as the Wars of the Roses re-ignited. In 1470–1, Edward was forced into exile and Henry VI was briefly declared king once more, before Edward returned to defeat and kill Warwick. The triumph of the House of York seemed complete.

But 12 years later in 1483, following Edward's death, his brother Richard seized the throne as Richard III, apparently having had Edward's sons Edward V and Richard killed. Richard III's reign lasted no more than two years: the Lancastrians returned to win a final victory – in the form of Henry Tudor, the grandson of Henry V's widow, Catherine of Valois, and great-grandson of John of Gaunt, Duke of Lancaster (1340–99).

EDWARD IV
1461–1470, 1471–1483

In the eyes of his subjects, Edward proved the justice of his claim to the throne and his fitness to govern by defeating a Lancastrian army under the Duke of Somerset at the Battle of Towton, in March 1461. With the Lancastrian cause in disarray and Queen Margaret having fled to Scotland, Edward was crowned with great ceremony on 28 June in Westminster Abbey.

AN UNDIPLOMATIC MARRIAGE

A proven warrior, Edward had little of his predecessor Henry VI's profound piety, instead exhibiting a strong liking for the pleasures of the flesh. Early in his reign he won himself a reputation as a

Below: King Edward had a taste for lavish clothes, made from the finest animal furs, velvet and cloth of gold.

Above: Physical authority. Powerfully built and 6ft 4in (1.93m) tall, Edward IV was both approachable and charismatic.

> **EDWARD IV, KING OF ENGLAND, 1461–1470, 1471–1483**
> **Birth:** 28 April 1442, Rouen, Normandy
> **Father:** Richard, Duke of York
> **Mother:** Cecily, Duchess of York
> **Accession:** 4 March 1461
> **Coronation:** 28 June 1461, Westminster Abbey
> **Queen:** Elizabeth Woodville (m. 1 May 1464; d. 1492)
> **Succeeded by:** His son Edward V
> **Greatest achievement:** Establishment of House of York
> **29 March 1461:** Battle of Towton
> **1470:** Flees into exile
> **14 April 1471:** Defeats Warwick the Kingmaker at Battle of Barnet
> **21 May 1471:** Reclaims throne
> **Death:** 9 April 1483, Windsor

womanizer. Indeed, Edward's weakness for beautiful women led to one of the major misjudgements of his reign: his secret marriage to Elizabeth Woodville, the widow of a Lancastrian nobleman who had been killed in the 1461 Battle of St Albans. The story goes that Edward met Elizabeth when he visited a castle during a hunting trip and was at once deeply taken with her looks. She resisted all his advances and declared that he would have to marry her in order to have what he wanted. Unable to resist her charms, Edward married Elizabeth in utmost secrecy in May 1464.

Edward's subjects felt that Elizabeth did not have the social status necessary to be queen. More importantly, the marriage angered Edward's great noble ally Warwick the Kingmaker, for Elizabeth imported her five brothers and seven sisters to the royal court and insisted that Edward shower them with favours that Warwick resented. In addition, Warwick was secretly in negotiations with King Louis of France, in which he had promised the king's hand in marriage to a French princess and these talks now came to nothing.

FORCED INTO EXILE

In 1469 Warwick inspired a revolt in Yorkshire against Edward. The rebels, fronted by 'Robin of Redesdale' (in reality close Warwick ally Sir John Conyers), defeated the king in battle. Edward was briefly imprisoned by Warwick before he was released and returned to the throne in London.

Then, in 1470, Edward was betrayed and forced into exile. Journeying to France, Warwick had allied himself with his former enemy Queen Margaret and with the king's brother, the Duke of Clarence. When Edward marched north to deal with further Warwick-inspired rebellions, Warwick and Clarence landed an army on the south coast with the intention of restoring Henry VI to the throne. Even then, Edward remained confident of his ability to see off his former mentor, but he was betrayed by the Marquis of Montagu who allied himself with Warwick and left the king so heavily outnumbered that he was forced to flee to exile in Burgundy. Warwick and Clarence took control, freed Henry VI

Below: Beguiled by beauty, Edward recklessly plunged into a secret marriage to Elizabeth Woodville in May 1464.

ENGLAND'S FIRST PRINTED BOOK

King Edward was a man of culture and taste as well as a warrior and political schemer. He financed the printing of the first dated book in English, which was also the first book printed in England.

The Dictes and Sayenges of the Phylosophers was printed by William Caxton in 1477. Caxton was a Kent-born merchant who flourished in Flanders and Holland and learned printing in Cologne in the early 1470s. He translated *The Recuyell of the Historyes of Troye* into English and printed it, but without a date, in Bruges, in 1475. The following year Caxton returned to London and set up his printing press in Westminster. He presented *The Dictes and Sayenges of the Phylosophers* to Edward in the year of its publication.

Left: This woodcut of a knight was used to illustrate Caxton's Game of the Chesse.

from the Tower of London, where he had been kept, and crowned him once more as King of England.

The revival of Henry's reign lasted no more than six months. Edward returned to England, made peace with Clarence, then defeated and killed Warwick and Montagu in battle at Barnet on 14 April 1471. Afterwards he returned Henry to imprisonment in the Tower.

In May he trounced the forces of Queen Margaret at Tewkesbury, capturing Margaret herself and beheading her prominent supporters, including the Duke of Somerset. Margaret's son Edward, the Prince of Wales, was killed as he tried to escape and shortly thereafter Henry VI died in mysterious circumstances. It is likely that he was killed, perhaps by Edward's brother Richard of Gloucester. The new king's victory seemed complete and the crown secure with the new House of York.

APPETITE FOR PLEASURE

Edward was a man of urgent appetites, who was rumoured to make himself vomit during banquets so he could continue to gorge on rich foods and who boasted that he had three mistresses, 'One the merriest, the other the wiliest, the third the holiest harlot in the

realm'. They included Elizabeth Shore, a London grocer's wife, and Elizabeth Lucy, daughter of a Hampshire nobleman and mother of a notable illegitmate son, Arthur Plantagenet.

Edward's overindulgence probably contributed to his sudden death, aged 40. In his later years he grew corpulent, and in March 1483 he was struck down by a mystery illness variously said to have been malaria, pneumonia or a stroke. He died on 9 April, 1483.

Below: Edward asserted his authority at Barnet in April 1471, killing the Marquis of Montagu and Earl of Warwick.

THE PRINCES IN THE TOWER

ROYAL MURDER, 1483

As Protector of the Kingdom in summer 1483, Richard Duke of Gloucester had the 12-year-old King Edward V and the king's brother Richard housed in the Tower Of London, which at that time was a palace as well as a jail. Shortly after Gloucester engineered his elevation to the throne, the princes disappeared and many assumed, then and since, that they had been murdered on Richard's orders. The question of what happened to the princes in the Tower is one of the most enduringly fascinating mysteries of English royal history.

THE PRINCES DISAPPEAR

Around the time of Gloucester's coronation as King Richard III on 6 July 1483, Edward and Richard were moved within the Tower of London complex from the royal apartments to the Garden Tower. They were seen playing with bows and arrows in the constable's garden close by. They were then moved again, to the White Tower, where many prison cells were situated. After this, they simply disappeared.

In the 16th century, Richard III was generally assumed to have been behind the princes' disappearance. Within weeks of their disappearance, the Venetian ambassador wrote home to say that the princes had been murdered on Richard's orders. It is certain that Richard had plenty to gain from their deaths. When he claimed the throne he justified it by declaring that the young King Edward V and his brother were illegitimate, since their father Edward IV's marriage to Queen Elizabeth Woodville had been invalid. He knew that if Edward lived

Below: Many romantic visions of the brothers were painted in the 19th century, including this one by Paul Delaroche.

Above: In 1878, Sir John Everett Millais pictured the princes caught like innocent animals with nowhere to run.

he would be a figurehead for rebellions. It was a common occurrence in the political-dynastic manoeuvrings of 14th- and 15th-century royal history for a deposed monarch to die, usually in captivity and in mysterious circumstances, shortly after losing power. This fate had befallen Edward II, and the case of Henry VI would have cautioned Richard against allowing the princes to live. Henry had remained a

THE BONES OF THE PRINCES?

In 1674, in the reign of King Charles II, two skeletons were discovered buried at the Tower of London. Judged to be the bones of the young princes, they were reinterred at Westminster Abbey. In 1993, scientists examined the bones and determined that they were the remains of males who had died in boyhood, consistent with the possibility that the skeletons were those of the young princes. However, the scientists were unable to find definitive proof that the skeletons were those of the ousted King Edward V and his brother.

figurehead for rebel discontent long after his deposition by Edward IV in 1461 and was even released from imprisonment to reoccupy the throne briefly in 1470. After that event, Henry VI himself met a mysterious death in May 1471, according to some reports at the hand of the future Richard III, at the time the brother of the ruling king, Edward IV.

CHARACTER ASSASSINATION?

Traditionally, Richard III has been seen as a cruel, treacherous and ruthlessly ambitious man, easily capable of dark deeds such as the murder of the boys, his life blighted by the success of his brother Edward IV and his own hunch-backed physique. However, this popular conception of the king's build and character derives from propaganda issued by the Tudors after Henry Tudor had taken Richard's crown at Bosworth in August 1485. Historians know, for example, that the idea of Richard being a hunchback – so familiar from Shakespeare's play *King Richard III* – was entirely an invention, and that he was broad-shouldered and 5 ft 8in (1.72m) in height, taller than most of his contemporaries.

Henry Tudor had as much, if not more, to gain from the death of young Edward V, for his own claim to the throne did not stand if Edward lived. It was squarely in his interests for the boys to disappear and for the blame to be cast on their uncle Richard. Henry was able to rally support for his attack on Richard by casting him as a scheming usurper, a murderer of the rightful king, young Edward.

THEORIES ASSESSED

According to one theory, the princes were still alive when Richard was defeated by Henry Tudor at Bosworth Field and lived on in captivity for around two years into the reign of Henry VII. At that time Henry decided they were a threat to his own position, and they were murdered. Another theory is that Henry, Duke of Buckingham

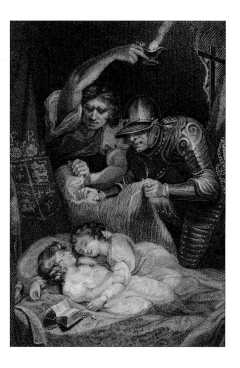

Above: Innocence betrayed. Another 19th-century view imagines the dark hour of the boys' murder by Richard III's henchmen.

was responsible for the deed. Buckingham, a former ally of Richard III, himself had a viable claim to the throne as a descendant of King Edward III; he was also a supporter of the cause of Henry Tudor. In killing the boys he could have been seeking to open the way to the throne either for himself or for Tudor.

On balance, however, it seems most likely that King Richard was responsible for the boys' deaths. Few people would claim that he killed them with his own hands. Sixteenth-century accounts indicated that Sir James Tyrell, carrying out the king's orders, hired two of the boys' keepers, Miles Forest and John Dighton, as assassins. They smothered the princes as they slept in their beds and afterwards buried their lifeless bodies in the grounds of the Tower.

According to the doctor who attended the boys in the Tower before their disappearance, Edward was living in fear that he might die at any time. The doctor relates that the doomed boy declared poignantly, 'I would my uncle would let me have my life though I lose my kingdom'.

EDWARD V AND RICHARD III

1483-1485

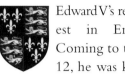 Edward V's reign is the shortest in English history. Coming to the throne aged 12, he was king for a mere two months and 17 days, from the death of his father Edward IV, on 9 April 1483, to the fateful day of 25 June, on which the boy-king's uncle Richard Duke of Gloucester accepted Parliament's request that he accede to the throne himself as King Richard III.

A ROYAL COUP

Gloucester engineered a coup. On his deathbed, Edward IV named Gloucester Protector of the Kingdom and guardian of young Prince Edward. The late king's widow, Queen Elizabeth Woodville, had other plans, however. She was determined to exclude Gloucester from power, to have her son crowned without delay and to surround him with members of the Woodville family, who were highly unpopular at court. She asked young Edward's guardian, Anthony Woodville, Earl Rivers, to

Below: The general image of King Richard is that of an ogre tormented by his sins, as presented in Shakespeare's Richard III.

EDWARD V, KING OF ENGLAND, 1483

Birth: 2 Nov 1470, the Sanctuary, Westminster Abbey
Father: Edward IV
Mother: Elizabeth Woodville
Accession: 9 April 1483
Deposed: 25 June 1483
Succeeded by: His uncle Richard III
Death: 3 Sept 1483. Probably murdered with his brother Richard, Duke of York, in the Tower

---

escort the prince from Ludlow Castle in Shropshire, where they were staying, to London for a coronation ceremony planned for 4 May. Gloucester, who was in Yorkshire at the time of Edward IV's death, travelled south to intervene.

Near Northampton on 30 April, Gloucester and his close ally Henry, Duke of Buckingham, arrested Rivers and the escort and took Prince Edward into their own care. Hearing the news, Queen Elizabeth took sanctuary in Westminster Abbey with her younger son, Richard, Duke of York.

In London, Gloucester became Protector on 6 May and rescheduled Edward's coronation for 22 June. He put Edward in the Tower of London. On 13 June he accused his former ally Lord Hastings of plotting against him and had him executed. Then he took the nine-year-old Duke of York from sanctuary in the Abbey and put him with his brother in the Tower. On 22 June he declared that the late king's secret marriage to Elizabeth Woodville was not valid and that the heir to the throne and his brother were illegitimate. On these grounds he declared himself the rightful inheritor of the crown. On 25 June Parliament backed Gloucester's claims and asked him to be king. He was crowned Richard III on 6 July.

Above: Edward V seemed destined for greatness on the throne. He was known for his charm, intelligence and good looks.

POLITICAL FALLOUT

The young princes officially remained in the Tower, but they were not seen after Richard III's coronation day. Increasingly, people were convinced that the princes were dead, probably murdered. When Richard's former ally Henry Stafford, Duke of Buckingham, rose in revolt in October, he assumed that the boys were dead and proposed that Richard be replaced on the throne

---

THE SAINTED MEMORY OF HENRY VI

In August 1484 King Richard III had the body of his predecessor Henry VI moved from Chertsey Abbey, where it was buried in 1471 after his unexplained death in the Tower of London, to a tomb in the choir of St George's Chapel, Windsor. There it lies, directly opposite the tomb of Richard's brother King Edward IV, who was Henry's rival in life. Henry VI was increasingly revered as a saintly figure, capable of working miracles for his supporters.

RICARDO · III

RICHARD III, KING OF ENGLAND, 1483–1485

Birth: 2 Oct 1452, Fotheringhay Castle, Northamptonshire

Father: Richard Plantagenet, Duke of York

Mother: Cecily Neville

Accession: 26 June 1483

Coronation: 6 July 1483

Queen: Anne Neville (m. 12 July 1472; d. 16 March 1485)

Succeeded by: Henry VII

Death: 22 Aug 1485 at the Battle of Bosworth Field, Lincs

Above: This 16th-century portrait follows chronicle accounts, which represent Richard III as thin-lipped, haggard and nervous.

by Henry Tudor, a descendant of Henry V's queen, Catherine of Valois and also a representative of the Lancastrian claim to the throne as the son of Margaret Beaufort, granddaughter of John of Gaunt. Henry prepared to invade England from exile in Brittany, but Buckingham was captured and executed on 2 November, and Henry retreated.

PERSONAL COSTS

The following year King Richard's 11-year-old son and only child, Edward, Prince of Wales, died. Richard and his queen, Anne, were maddened with grief. The prospect of a Yorkist inheritance, so dear to Richard's heart, began to look extremely vulnerable and when, in March 1485, Queen Anne died after a prolonged illness, rumours circulated that Richard had had her killed so that he could bolster his position by marrying his niece, Elizabeth of York.

In the event, Yorkist rule would only last a further five months. Henry Tudor won the backing of King Charles VIII of France as well as of Queen Elizabeth and the Woodville camp for his claim to the throne.

BOSWORTH FIELD

Henry encountered Richard's army at Market Bosworth on 22 August. The encounter was decided by the king's desperate attack to try and bring the battle to a quick conclusion, which threw away a position of strength. As Richard watched the vanguard of his army take on the vanguard of Henry's, he had plenty of strength in reserve. However, in the distance he saw Henry Tudor's standard defended by only a few score troops and decided to attack, in the hope of bringing the clash to an early end by killing Henry.

At first the onslaught was successful and Richard himself killed several of Henry's bodyguards. When his own horse was slain beneath him he fought on, on foot. At this point Sir William Stanley threw his men into an attack on the king. Richard was killed, his body stripped and slung naked across a horse. Henry Tudor left Bosworth Field wearing the crown he had won.

Below: In August 1485, the succession was decided at Bosworth. Richard III fought bravely, if recklessly, in his final battle.

INDEX

PICTURE ACKNOWLEDGEMENTS

Alamy: /BEP 51t /Bildarchiv Monheim GmbH 47b, 85b /Bill Bachmann 64br /Kathy deWitt 36t /Elmtree Images 49tl /gkphotography 71b /Iconotec 62b /Pawel Libera 8b /David Robertson 64bl /Worldwide Picture Library 61t
The Ancient Art & Architecture Collection: 8t, 18-19, 20tl&tr, 21t&b, 22b, 23bl, 29br, 31cr, 48, 58, 59bl&br
The Art Archive: 16b, 32, 33bl, 35, 43t, 46, 53, 70, 84t, 85t, /Ashmolean Museum, Oxford 27b /Biblioteca Nazionale, Turin /Dagli Orti 22t /Bibliotheque Municapale Dijon/Dagli Orti 23br /Bibliotheque Nationale, Paris: 52t, 83b; /Bodleian Library, Oxford 16t, 25, 26t, 33br, 49b, 62t,

74b /British Library 2, 9tl&tr, 17bl, 24br, 28, 36b, 38-9, 40, 42t&b, 54, 55b, 69t, 88b /British Library/HarperCollins Publishers 17t, 44 /British Library/Eileen Tweedy 24bl, 80bl /Dagli Orti 17br, 6–7, 41, 50t /Guildhall Library/ Eileen Tweedy 66t /Jarrold Publishing 9b, 26b, 45t, 50b /Musée de la Tapisserie, Bayeux/Dagli Orti 33t, 34 /Musée de Louvre, Paris/Dagli Orti 90 /Musée du Château de Versailles/ Dagli Orti 52b, 76t /Musée Saint Denis, Reims/ Dagli Orti 60t /Musée Thomas Dobree, Nantes/Dagli Orti 84b, 86b /National Gallery/ Eileen Tweedy 55t /San Carlos Museum, Mexico City/Dagli Orti 73tr

The Bridgeman Art Library: /British Library, London 29bl, 31b, 78-9, 81tl, 82, 87 /Centrale Bibliotheek van de Universiteit, Ghent, Belgium 89br /Chetham's Library, Manchester 37 /Falkland Palace, Falkland, Fife 56-7 /Fitzwilliam Museum, University of Cambridge 77c&cr /Gloucester Cathedral, Glos/Paul Maeyaert 51b /Houses of Parliament, Westminster 86t /Lambeth Palace Library, London 31t /Lincolnshire County Council, Usher Gallery 76b /The Illustrated London News Picture Library, London, 10t /National Gallery of Scotland, Edinburgh 67 /National Library of Scotland, Edinburgh 68b&t, 69b, 72t /Private Collection 27t, 80br, 89bl, 93b /Private Collection, Philip Mould,

Historical Portraits Ltd, London 77br, 81tr, 93t /Private Collection, The Stapleton Collection 60b, 92t /Private Collection, Ken Welsh 91tr /Royal Holloway, University of London 91tl /Scottish National Portrait Gallery, Edinburgh 72b, 73tl, 74t /Society of Antiquaries, London 88t /Worcester Cathedral, Worcs 45b
Mary Evans Picture Library: 43b, 47t, 61bl&bc, 64t, 65t, 71t, 75t&b, 89t, 92b
Joy Wotton 1, 11t